BROKEN
BEYOND
RECOGNITION

BEAUTY FROM ASHES

KATHERINE ELAM SIMPSON

Largo, MD

Copyright © 2020 Katherine Elam Simpson

All rights reserved under the international copyright law. No part of this book may be reproduced or transmitted in any form or by any means, electronic or mechanical, including photocopying, recording, or by any information storage and retrieval system, without the express, written permission of the publisher or the author. The exception is reviewers, who may quote brief passages in a review.

ISBN 9781562293734

Christian Living Books, Inc.
P. O. Box 7584
Largo, MD 20792
christianlivingbooks.com
We bring your dreams to fruition.

Unless otherwise noted, Scripture quotations are taken from the King James Version of the Bible. Scripture quotations marked ESV are taken from The ESV® Bible (The Holy Bible, English Standard Version®), Copyright © 2001 by Crossway, a publishing ministry of Good News Publishers. Used by permission. All rights reserved. Scripture quotations marked NIV are taken from the Holy Bible, New International Version®, NIV®. Copyright © 1973, 1978, 1984, 2011 by Biblica, Inc.® Used by permission of Zondervan. All rights reserved worldwide. Scripture quotations marked NLT are taken from the Holy Bible, New Living Translation, Copyright © 1996, 2004, 2007 by Tyndale House Foundation. Used by permission of Tyndale House Publishers, Inc. All rights reserved.

Library of Congress Cataloging-in-Publication Data

Names: Simpson, Katherine Elam, author.
Title: Broken beyond recognition : beauty from ashes / Katherine Elam Simpson.
Description: Largo, MD : Christian Living Books, 2020.
Identifiers: LCCN 2020024895 | ISBN 9781562293888 (paperback) |
  ISBN 9781562293895 (ebook)
Subjects: LCSH: Simpson, Katherine Elam. | Christian biography. | African
  American women--Biography. | African American Christians--California
  --Los Angeles--Biography. | Child abuse--California--Los Angeles--Biography.
Classification: LCC BR1725.S46765 A3 2020 | DDC 277.308/3092 [B]--dc23
LC record available at https://lccn.loc.gov/2020024895

ENDORSEMENTS

Katherine's journey expresses the prophetic revelation of coming out of the wilderness. Right words and right choices give us the opportunity to be truly free. I believe this book is a catalyst for transformation.

JOHN HARKE
Passion Ministries

This book is indicative of the transforming power of God. It reaches into the psychology of men in ways that traditional psychiatric therapy falls short: a microcosm of the depth of divine grace.

DR. G.E. LASSITER SR.
Pastor, Love Unlimited Church

This book describes the amazing journey of an incredible leader in the kingdom of God. Katherine is by far one of the most influential leaders, powerful speakers, and progressive thinkers and writers to emerge over the last twenty years. Her journey will bless, inspire, and give you hope. Congratulations, Katherine!

BISHOP JOHN MARK RICHARDSON SR.
Prelate, New Journey Jurisdiction Church of God in Christ

This is a great book. If you are unhappy and looking for peace and joy, read it. It will give you a new outlook on life and lift you out of darkness into light.

CARDELL CANDLER
Elder, Trinity Chapel Life Center

May the life-giving theme of this book rebuild, repair, restore, and bring wholeness to your life as you read about the miraculous transformation found in Jesus Christ.

CHERIE CANDLER
Trinity Chapel Life Center

This is an incredibly unique, thoughtful, and powerful gift to help individuals overcome real-life obstacles by deepening their spiritual relationships. Katherine is the example of someone who took control and claimed her life, proving that you are not your past. If you or someone you know is struggling with life's downfalls and feel as if there is no hope, read this book.

JOE CLARKE
Director of Commercial Real Estate
M.E. Properties Beverly Hills

The author of this life-changing book has gained wisdom beyond her years through the many trials and tribulations in her life. However, through it all, this powerhouse of a woman has kept her faith and an unquenchable thirst for helping people get healed all over the world. This book is a must-read game changer!

DR. JILL ELAM
Doctor of Social Work

This phenomenal book is guaranteed to touch countless lives as you directly experience God's exchange of ashes for beauty. My spiritual mother is one of God's greatest, most admirable spirits. I love and salute you!

EVANGELIST SHARREL JOHNSON
New Region For Christ

Congratulations on such a phenomenal book. It will impact the life of each reader due to the relevance of its content. I am godly proud to say I am one of the former Women Waving the Banner of Freedom daughters spoken about in this book. This book will reach audiences of all ages and walks of life as it provides the necessary tools to face and conquer life's obstacles and mishaps. I love you, Mom.

DR. KELINDA RICE
Kingdom Faith Ministries Intl. Inc
Houston, Texas

Authenticity of truth is revealed in this book. It takes real courage to reveal the truth that exposes at the expense of helping others to be free. What an awesome and unselfish display of ministry in this writing that I'm sure will set the captives free. Congratulations to you as you are the blessed of God.

APOSTLE REGINALD D. RICE SR.
Founder of Kingdom Faith Ministries Intl. Inc.

Katherine is a person of excellence, energy, and godly character. I have always seen her encouraging people to be their best. Over the years, I have been a witness to both her growth and success. This book is going to transform many people's lives for the better.

PASTOR EDWARD ROBINSON JR.
Trinity Chapel Life Center

Great congratulations are in order to the readers of this awesome encounter. Katherine impacted my life for over ten years. She is a spiritual mother who strives to model her life after the likeness of Christ. Her story is about moving from tragedy to triumph.

It will inspire you in ways where you too will be triumphant. It's a must-read.

PROPHETESS ANEESHA M. ROSS, MBA

When you are hurting and your heart cries out, where do you go? Katherine takes you on a journey through the storms of life and leads you into the light and love of the sovereign God.

REGGIE SPEARMAN
Pastor of Visitation
Faithful Central Bible Church

When we create and work for the new and push ourselves ahead in search of fulfillment and change, we do so in collective progress. Then we step into the unknown together, ready to shape what's coming. I'm so proud to be in the life of my kingdom sister and co-laborer as she transparently shares her life, walk, preaching, ministry, and display of God's love revealing the secret of her suffering. Who better than she? I love you, my sister, cousin, and co-laborer!

PASTOR LISA MACKEY WALTON
Lisa Mackey Walton Ministries Inc.

My hero, my strength, my mother! Words cannot describe how proud I am that you're sharing *your story*. This book is going to help and inspire so many broken people, not just women. I love you, and I'm very grateful God chose you to be my mother. Keep thriving, "Eagle," as you tell us!

KIERRA "KITKAT" WASHINGTON
Owner of Do You Salon

DEDICATION

This book is dedicated to the lover of my soul, Jesus Christ. I am nothing without You! You are the reason I live. I will live for all eternity with You. Thank You, Lord, for giving me beauty for ashes and breaking me beyond recognition to produce a better me. Your unconditional love has healed my wounds and left no scars. Today I walk in an attitude of gratitude for the things You have done. I love You forever!

CONTENTS

Foreword   xi
Introduction   xiii

1	Watts Up, Girl…!	1
2	Too Much for Her Little Eyes	9
3	The Seed Was Planted	27
4	Who Am I Becoming?	41
5	If You Get Me Out of This One	55
6	I Can't Breathe	63
7	Wrong Rib	77
8	He Found His Good Thing Wounded	83
9	The Invites Just Wouldn't Stop	93
10	Don't Lose Your Mind; You're Gonna Need It	105
11	Destiny's Daughter	111
12	Take the Women to the Well	119
13	Broken Beyond Recognition	135
14	He Gave Me Beauty. I Gave Him Ashes	145
15	You Can Make It! I Did	151

Special Acknowledgments   155
Acknowledgments   159
The Five Who Survived   161
About the Author   163

FOREWORD

This book immediately draws the reader in with a wow. Lady Simpson reflects on her life of brokenness. She candidly discloses her truth of growing up in a dysfunctional family. Later, her life is wrapped in dysfunction differently. The layers of abandonment, pain, rejection, and confusion may make it seem as if there is no hope.

The enemy is a master strategist at planting illusions and deceptions in our thoughts. Those illusions can trap you in a prison of yesterday's misfortunes. The enemy of our past has the nerve to catapult into our future suggesting that we settle and remain stuck. This book reveals content that many would never share. However, freedom and victory are beautiful. I can't help but laugh, for Lady Simpson secures recognition later by God.

It is often the pitiful heartaches and horrific memories that shatter many lives starting from when we are young. Grace is so powerful throughout this entire book. She gives hope and encouragement to those who are still in bondage by sharing her journey. It is a must-read and a page-turner. I was captivated with emotion while reading and was tremendously blessed.

I encourage you to look at your life and reflect on areas that call for complete healing and deliverance. *Broken Beyond Recognition* will empower you to speak your truth to become completely free. As Lady Simpson says, "You can make it! I did." God is a God of recompense; you too can receive beauty from ashes. That's good news.

LADY VICKI KEMP
Bestselling author of *Better than Yesterday*

INTRODUCTION

I am extremely honored and humbled that God chose me to write this book. According to statistics, someone coming from my background is not supposed to be an author. But to God be the glory. I have defeated the odds of illiteracy, alcoholism, prostitution, drug abuse, physical abuse, mental abuse, childhood trauma, and a hood rich with pride.

I wrote this book to help you understand the greatness God has placed in all of us and to let you know no opposition can stop it! Every time you are attacked, hit hard, and hurt, God will heal and restore you. In this book, I am very transparent and honest about my life journey and brokenness. I hope my story will inspire you to see that if God changed me, He can do it for you as well.

I do not intend in any way, form, or fashion to glorify my past lifestyle in this book. However, I am candid about it because it is the vehicle for my destiny. Ultimately, I hope this book demonstrates the power of God's amazing redemption plan for my life before the foundation of the world. In spite of the many roadblocks and obstacles that were set up to destroy me, I made it through them all. You can too! Your past does not have to dictate your future, no matter what it looks like.

Have you felt like giving up on life because of the severe, unbearable pain it has caused you? Have you been disappointed by the people closest to you, the ones you trusted most? Are you dealing with childhood trauma as an adult? If you have answered yes, this book is for you. It is also written for those trying to sedate their problems by using drugs and alcohol, those who never feel smart enough to accomplish anything, those looking for love in all the wrong places, and those who have lost children and played the "what if" game repeatedly.

If you are a woman who has used your body in degrading ways to make money or a drug dealer behind the jailhouse bars wondering how you got there, you were also on my mind when I was writing. Or perhaps you are the fly girl looking good on the outside, dripping with diamonds and pearls, wearing nothing but the finest designer labels. You parade through life with a mask of pride and arrogance, but on the inside you are empty and spiritually void; I've got you too.

ALSO AVAILABLE

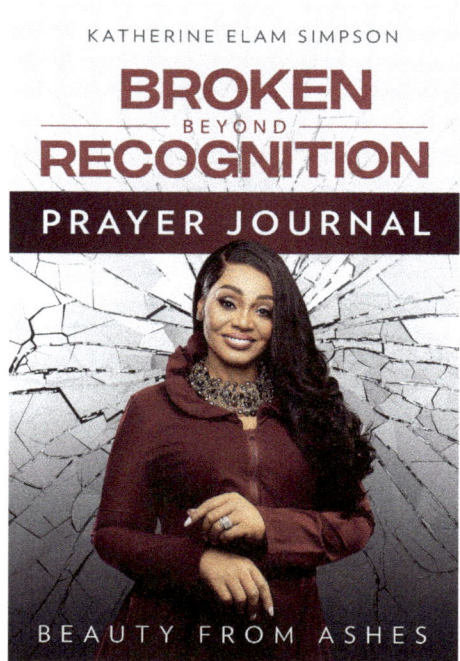

Broken Beyond Recognition Prayer Journal
ISBN 9781562293932 | 6"x9" | Paperback | 180 pages | $14.99
Available wherever books are sold and from
ChristianLivingBooks.com

CHAPTER 1

WATTS UP, GIRL…!

Watts will always hold a very special place in my heart. I call it the school of hard knocks. However, although growing up in Watts, California, was very challenging at times, it was not always bad. I had some really good times in Watts, even with its many lessons to be learned. I often say if you survive living in Watts, you have graduated from the school of the gladiators!

In the '60s, '70s, and '80s, Watts was a place of family, love, music, style, arts, culture, creativity, and lots of soul food. It was a neighborhood where families knew and respected one another. People actually cared about each other's wellbeing.

As the years progressed, life slowly changed. Drugs and gangs infiltrated our community and destroyed its very essence. The morals and values my grandparents taught me no longer seemed to exist. They taught my siblings and me to always respect our elders. We couldn't call our adult neighbors by their first names. We had to use their last names preceded by Mr. or Mrs. If our neighbors saw us doing something wrong, they had the right to correct, chastise, and take us home to our parents where we would get a second dose of chastisement. My grandmother Big Mama would say, "It's all in love. You may not understand it now, but one day you will." Later in life, I understood they were actually trying to prevent us from going the wrong way.

Growing up in Watts was amazing. We weren't millionaires, but we were rich in creativity. We would make our own clothes, styles, and dances. Interestingly, we would frequently see our creations on TV. That's right. Celebrities wore our styles. They danced the dances we choreographed right in our front yards while playing around. It was obvious someone was watching these little kids in the ghetto and robbing us of our creativity.

Watts Festival

In the '60s and '70s, the Watts Summer Festival was the place to be. Once a year, Will Rogers Park on 103rd Street was transformed into a wildly exciting festival full of black culture, soul food, music, games, and lots of carnival rides. Everyone came to the Watts festival. People traveled from all the surrounding cities near and far to have a good time. The beautiful dashiki outfits and afros of those walking around created a kaleidoscope of colors. The place was crowded with wonderful people who had a genuine love for culture and others. But amidst the happiness and grandeur of the festival, there were those who caused problems.

I recall one specific time when I was about seven years old. I was walking with my grandmother and siblings at the Watts festival in the nighttime. As we strolled down 103rd Street packed with people everywhere, I began to lag behind. I was captivated by all the excitement. Suddenly, a strange man grabbed me, turned me around, and started to walk me in the opposite direction of my family. Immediately, I screamed at the top of my voice. One of my siblings turned around and shouted, "It's Kathy!" They noticed I was snatched, and my grandmother ran back screaming my name, "Kathy! Kathy! Kathy!" The man let me go and ran off. Wow! After that experience, they never had to worry about me lagging behind anymore.

Our Watts parades were also amazing. We were proud of them. Full marching bands, drill teams, dressed-up horses and black cowboys, firemen, the mayor of the city, a celebrity or two, and lots of beautiful floats made up the lively procession. We all stood on the sidelines of 103rd Street watching them parade. Oftentimes we were very proud of our family members who were involved. We would shout out their names and take several pictures as they marched by.

Christmas in Watts

Christmas in Watts was a phenomenon in itself. It was so much fun. This was the time of year I *had* to be at my grandparents' house. My Creole grandmother from Louisiana would make a huge pot of Creole gumbo and rice. We were given candy canes, stockings full of fruit, and some hot homemade eggnog. Although we never got many gifts, we made the best of it.

The most exciting part was meeting up with all my cousins and neighborhood friends on 113th Street and Wilmington. We would open our gifts, pull out that big red and white box, put on those Street King skates, and head to Grape Street Elementary playground. There, we would skate and dance to the music blasting from the record shop across the street. It was so much fun; we could just dance on our skates all day! Back then, we thoroughly enjoyed being outside. We would make most of our toys, like taking old cart boxes, nailing old skates to the bottom, and calling them our go-carts. We loved jumping rope, playing jacks, and hopscotch. Most times, we would stay outside until the streetlights came on. That was our signal it was time to make our way home to get a big bowl of my grandmother's delicious gumbo.

In Watts, neighbors had plenty of fruit trees in their yards. Actually, every house had a different fruit tree, and we would organize a produce market on 113th Street to sell the fruits. However, it wasn't always perfect. Back in those days, we had fights with one another, but it was just that—fights. After the fight was over, we would pick up our belongings and go about our business. No one was shot or killed. But as time went on, things changed.

Everything was much less expensive in those days. You could even get penny candies. We would get lots of Jolly Ranchers, boil them in a pot until they were soft, smash them all together with a stainless-steel spoon, and make a giant lollipop. We also liked buying whole pickles from the meat market, biting the tops off, and sticking wine candies or peppermint sticks inside them. That was so delicious. Soul food places like Jordan Cafe, Smith BBQ, Emily's Burritos, Guts Burger, Lee's Market, Joe's Store, Tommy's Liquor Store, the Mirror Motel, Mufundi after-school arts programs, the Pink store back in the Imperial courts, and many other wonderful mom-and-pop businesses provided services to the community.

Drugs and gangs infiltrated our community and destroyed its very essence.

The Black Panthers

Oftentimes, on our way to school in the morning, the Black Panthers had a breakfast program. They had houses everywhere. One was on the corner of 113th Street where my grandparents lived just a few houses down. The Black Panthers would invite all the kids in the neighborhood to come and eat breakfast before school at their house. My siblings and I would always accept the invitation. For most of us kids, that was all the food we had. Also, it was also a chance for us to see all the guns they had on the wall in a glass showcase. Intimidating and frightening are the best ways I can describe the experience. But as a child, I wanted to eat!

The breakfast was delicious and healthy. After filling our tummies, the Black Panthers would say, "Now, go get your education, little sisters and brothers." Fed and inspired, we would walk out the door to be greeted by policemen slowly driving by with intense looks on their faces. I remember asking my brother Ronnie why the police didn't like the Black Panthers. I couldn't understand because they were doing good things for the community. But it was much deeper than my brother and I could see.

The Infamous Riot

In those days, we could shop on 103rd Street because there were plenty of stores, such as the Hudson Shoe Store and ABC Grocery Market. Many black-owned businesses lined this street. There were also plenty of tailors for the guys to get their suits made. Unfortunately, in 1965, the Watts riot destroyed most of the black businesses.

I still remember the smell of smoke and flames of fire everywhere. I recall the police cars as they flooded our communities. Police officers were hitting black people with billy clubs. As kids, we were ignorantly making up dances and shouting, "Burn, baby, burn!" However, my grandmother wouldn't have it. She immediately took offense and warned us to stop. She said in her wisdom, "It is our community that's burning, and tomorrow we will have nowhere to shop." And, oh, how right she was.

Shortly after she scolded us, my father ran up to my grandmother's house with blood gushing out of his hand. He had gotten cut with glass. He ran into the bathroom to wash the blood off. It looked as if he had been in a bad fight. I thought he was going to die. With blood dripping down the halls of my grandparents' house, my father wrapped his hand and headed back out into the riot.

Watts was a desolate dry place as we tried to recover from the ashes.

Days later, Watts was a very desolate and dry place as we tried to recover from the ashes. Small business owners swept in front of their little mom-and-pop stores with much despair and hopelessness in their eyes. Today I tell young people don't look at rioting as a solution. It resolves nothing. I tell young people if they are angry and feel discriminated against, protest peacefully. Write a petition, and above all, pray because prayer changes everything.

The Treasure of the Tower

Finally, we had our prized possession: the Watts Tower, which is still standing there today. As a child, my grandmother told me the story about a man named Simon Rodia who would walk the neighborhood pushing a basket/cart asking the residents for broken pieces of glass, cups, plates, and jars. He would accept anything that was glass. My grandmother said at first she was a little suspicious of what he was doing with all those broken glass pieces. But one day it was revealed he was building a tower right in the middle of Watts: a big, beautiful, tall tower.

Everyone was invited to see what he called the "Watts Tower." This masterful work of art was built with all the broken pieces donated by Watts residents. It became a central focus for Watts. Regularly, a friend and I would swing and play on the Watts Tower. It gave us all a sense of pride. Mr. Rodia took all our broken pieces and made a masterpiece out of them.

I really had lots of enjoyable days at my grandparents' house, but at my house—that was a different story. Life will prepare you for the good, bad, and ugly.

The Watts Tower is a U.S. National Historic Landmark

CHAPTER 2

TOO MUCH FOR HER LITTLE EYES

Living with my parents was quite different from what I experienced at my grandmother's house whenever we went to visit. My early years with my parents were extremely hard. They were young teens in love trying to raise five children: Ronald, Katherine, Antoinette, Cynthia, and Louis, three girls and two boys. I love my siblings dearly. Through it all, it was our love for each other that held us together. For us, the struggle has always been real!

I believe our parents really loved us and each other. Oftentimes they would sit in the middle of the floor at my grandparents' house and sing "Close Your Eyes" by Peaches & Herb to one another. They worked hard to provide for their five children. But one day, my father was shot by one of his close friends. Our lives changed forever as he fought to recover.

Somewhere along their journey of being young and inexperienced with five children, life became overwhelming. My parents looked to alcohol as a way to escape. Alcoholism is a disease that has plagued so many families just as it did ours. This disease caused my parents to make some very poor choices. Consequently, our home was a disrupted and horrifying place to live. The environment was not fit for any child to be raised in because the foundation was collapsing and falling apart.

Helpless and Afraid

My parents argued and fought all the time. When I was about five years old, I was petrified seeing them fight. I was so scared; I would run and hide in the closet with my hands covering my ears as I cried. Parents make the error of arguing and fighting right in front of children as if they are not there. This makes the children feel helpless and afraid. It can be traumatizing and something that lives with you for years until you receive help. I have come to understand that most of my poor choices in life were directly stimulated by my childhood trauma.

My mother was a promiscuous woman who lost her mother at a very young age. Not understanding much about parenting, she married my father when they were both quite young.

Me at five years old in kindergarten

She was only fifteen and beautiful with a very giving heart. She worked a few jobs but none for long. My mother loved to dance and party and was very good at styling hair.

My father was seventeen when he married my mother. My auntie once told me they were so young my maternal grandfather and paternal grandparents had to sign for them to get married. Dad was a handsome, hardworking man. I remember him driving trucks to the Long Beach dumpster trying to make money for his family. He loved having fun but was very temperamental. His roaming eyes lusted after women other than my mother.

Somewhere along their journey, life became overwhelming.

The Horrible Cycle

The drinking and fighting between my parents became more frequent in our home. It reached the point where I expected one to break out every day once they drank alcohol. My mother would always get the worst of it. Seeing her with black, swollen eyes, her teeth knocked out, and bruises on her body was too much for my little eyes. I can recall smelling the blood on the wet rag with ice chips she used to reduce the swelling on her face.

I can still see the hot flaming clothes hanger burning on the stove as my father threatened to beat my mother with it as she cried. I also remember him drawing back a hammer as he pressed her hands on the table and threatened to hit her fingers with it. Afterward, she would cry and scream, "I'm leaving him! I'm tired of this! I'm leaving!" Yes, at times she did leave. But he would always find her and beat her all the way back. Strangely enough, sometimes she would just come back. The abusive cycle would start all over again.

Of course, because of her absence, my siblings and I would be dragged to and fro. However, I could never figure out why she would return. Their drinking habit had become obvious.

So many times, my siblings and I would go without life's necessities. We would be hungry and cold because most of their money was now being spent on alcohol. Our house often smelled like Gallo White Port wine and Thunderbird. The scent was embedded into the fibers of our home.

No bills were being paid, so very often we would have no electricity. If we had lights, we had no gas. At times we would be so hungry we would go into the backyard, pick green peaches from the tree, and eat them until we were full—only to get a bad stomachache. Sometimes the hunger would be so unbearable that when my parents left home, I would ask the neighbors if we could borrow a cup of sugar, flour, butter, and eggs—anything we could get our hands on to make a meal. Being the oldest girl, I felt a sense of responsibility to help my oldest brother Ronnie provide.

Other times we would get a cup and scrape the ice from the refrigerator to eat. Once in a while we even used our tongues. Sometimes our tongues would get stuck on the ice. How painful was that? Someone would have to run and get water to pour on our stuck tongues to unstick them. I don't know if you have ever been so hungry that you picked out the fried pieces of leftover crumbs from the grease on the stove. We had to do that several times.

Jamie

I recall that one day my father took my siblings and me to a pet store on Alameda to buy us a pet of our choice. We thought it was very nice of him. So my siblings and I chose a beautiful white rabbit and named her Jamie. We were so excited about our beautiful rabbit.

Every day we would play and talk to Jamie. We enjoyed seeing her run around the house, but after a few months Jamie would get away and run down the street. One day, after coming home from school and playing outdoors, we couldn't find Jamie.

My father called my siblings and me into the house for dinner. We sat there thinking how nice of him and how delicious the meal smelled. Gravy rice and chicken—this was rare, but we were so happy to have a meal. Then one of my siblings asked where Jamie was. Instead of answering, our father said, "Eat your food!" Whatever my father said, you did it! So we ate. Then our father said something that devastated my siblings and me for years. He said, "The meat you are eating is Jamie." Instantly, all five of us began to throw up on our plates. We cried loudly because Jamie was never coming back. Yet it meant nothing to our father. From a child, he was accustomed to killing chickens and eating them. But we were hurt because Jamie's white fur was in the backyard trash. That night, all five of us went to bed hungry once again because we refused to eat Jamie.

Child Labor

My oldest brother Ronald was always very smart. He was the mastermind behind our plans. He became our provider at nine years old, doing favors for people in the neighborhood. He would cut their grass and clean their yards. If he had no work, I would hold up the hood of cars while he got the battery out, so we could sell it and get food. Sorry, but we were in survival mode as little children. Whatever we could do to get money to feed our siblings and each other, we did it. Today, when I see young children begging for food or money, I know straightaway they are in survival mode. Children who are well taken care of don't beg for food and money.

> Ronald became our provider doing favors for people in the neighborhood.

Sometimes when our parents left us home alone, my brother and I would lock our siblings up safely in the house. We would go to the Alameda train tracks, pick up aluminum and scrap iron pieces, put them in a bucket, and take them to the steel mill yard to sell. We were paid $5 if we had enough, which was a lot of money back then. From our earnings, we would buy cans of pork 'n' beans and bread from the liquor store to feed our siblings. We were only about eight and nine years old.

We would hide the money from our parents. One time my oldest brother and I made $5 working on the train tracks. We were so happy and proud of ourselves that we told our parents we had earned $5. But to our surprise, they took it away to buy more alcohol. We learned to keep our mouths shut about the money we made.

We often missed school because our parents had hangovers from drinking and partying all night. It was hard to go to school the next day because our home was filled with strangers and loud music the night before. Sometimes in the morning, we would have to step over strangers to get ready for school. We had no clean clothes or hot meals. Our parents were too hungover to care. As the oldest girl, I was left to comb my sisters' hair and dress them for school. I would dig through dirty clothes trying to find them something to wear. Most of the time if I did get to school, I would be late.

The Struggle Was Real

I couldn't stay focused on my education because of all the turmoil going on at home. I used school for free breakfast and lunch, but my grades were very poor. I struggled with reading, writing, and spelling. My teacher would say, "Katherine, read chapter one in our textbook." Oh, no, I would think to myself. I can't read like the other kids. I would just die inside from embarrassment.

There was no one at home to help me learn. Maybe if I didn't have to try being an adult before my time, I could have learned. Instead, I was made fun of and talked about. What I really wanted to tell my teacher and classmates was, "I'm really smart. I just need help. My parents are alcoholics." I now understand that the first few years of a child's life are some of the most important. In fact, about 80 percent of a child's brain is developed by age three with a key period of development occurring in their language and literacy skills.

I really struggled hard in elementary school, not only with reading, writing, and spelling but with the students as well. Some of my classmates were very cruel. My teacher would ask all of us to remove our shoes and sit on the floor with our legs crossed. I would not remove my shoes because I knew my socks were dirty and had lots of holes in them. One day she said, "Katherine, remove your shoes." I continued to sit there, but she came over and took them off. All the kids laughed and made fun of my dirty, smelly socks. What they didn't know was I was trying to survive in a house of horror.

When I got home from school, my father would take my siblings and me to the back of store dumpsters to sort through the garbage looking for edible food; that would be our dinner for the day. I would often wonder why we had to be in the dumpster when others were shopping inside the store. Nevertheless, even as a child, I never gave up on looking for better days. I didn't know when or how. All I knew was if others could live well, one day I would too.

Say Something

As time went on, the fighting and abuse included the children. My father slapped me so hard one day when I was about nine or ten years old that the entire side of my face went numb; my ears were ringing. Being slapped with full force by your father is devastating and dehumanizing. He did it simply because I forgot to do something he had asked me to do. Soon the abuse of my siblings and me escalated. By this time, my father was bringing home his mistresses. My mother couldn't say anything to him about it. She would get really mad and tell us, "That's your daddy's girlfriends, Flo and Mary." And I would be thinking, I thought you were the girlfriend.

Still, no one seemed to notice that five children were suffering in this house of horror. We were being abused and neglected, but no one seemed to care. Perhaps people were just minding their own business. Anytime a child is being neglected and mistreated, it should become everyone's business and concern. Even now, some would prefer if I didn't tell this truth! But to you, I say, "You didn't live in that house of horror with my siblings and me, so you have no right to say what I should or shouldn't share." I hope this book motivates others who see children being abused or neglected to come forward and get help for them.

My father developed a very bad cough that lingered for weeks and weeks. It was not getting better but worse. He wasn't working, and the only income was the county check my mother was receiving for the five of us. My father decided to take the money, drive to Mexico to purchase vases, and bring them back to sell. I could see at times he wanted to pull out of the depression and addiction to alcohol, but it had such a strong hold on him. He became very bitter, angry, and temperamental with everyone around him. His plan to sell vases was great but the execution all wrong. He took my mother and the two oldest children: my older brother and me. That meant my youngest siblings, ages two to seven years old, were left at home alone for three days. They were standing on the front porch crying as my father instructed them to go back into the house and lock the door. I could see they were scared, but no one dared to tell my father no. That was something you just didn't do. You just did what he said.

We were on the road to Mexico for what seemed like days, not a few hours. The car was not in the best of shape; it was an old white Dodge. The windows wouldn't roll all the way up, and it was cold. My brother and I were in the backseat looking out the window. All I saw were lots of dirt hills and mountains. My mother was sleeping in the front seat, and my dad was driving. I could not stop thinking about my siblings who were home alone. Who was going to care for them? How would they eat? Would I ever see them again? We seemed so far away from them.

Suddenly, it happened. The car tumbled over and over as my brother and I were being tossed around the backseat. Our mother was screaming, "Louis, wake up!" He had fallen asleep behind the wheel and the car was flipping out of control. It landed upside down with smoke coming from everywhere. All I could think was I didn't want to die! People screamed through the windows of our car as we were upside down. "Do you need help? Are you OK?" My father replied, "Yes, we need help to get out!" The strangers helped all of us to get out safely and gave us a ride to the nearest bus station. The car had to be junked. It was totally destroyed. But we continued to Mexico. I remember getting off the bus in Mexico as little kids ran up to us asking for money. That was the first time I had seen kids who seemed to be as bad off as we were.

My father purchased several cheap vases in Mexico. We were loaded down with them on our return to the bus station. By the time we got on the bus, we were exhausted. Unfortunately, one by one, the vases started cracking. We purchased ten vases, but by the time we got home, we only had about three.

My brother and I were so glad to make it back home to see our siblings alive. Looking back now, all I can say is God has always had His hand on the five of us. The mental and physical abuse should have taken us out. But it didn't.

The abuse should have taken us out. But it didn't.

Although the cough my father had was not improving but getting even worse, he wouldn't go to the hospital. He told my mother he was throwing up blood and there was blood in his stool, but he still wouldn't seek help. His birthday was drawing near, so my grandparents, aunties, and uncles decided to give him a birthday party at my grandmother's house. I was so excited! Not about the birthday party but because I loved going to my grandmother's house; my grandparents were always kind to us. They would always ask us if we were hungry, but my mother and father would say no, we had just eaten, which was not true. However, as soon as our parents turned their backs, my siblings and I would have a feast. We would eat up everything.

113th Street

I was also excited about the party because it would give me a chance to see my auntie Yolanda and my cousin Sandra. We were more like sisters. I could also see some friends. 113th and Wilmington was where the Elams lived. We were well-known in the neighborhood, and if you messed with one of us, you had to fight all of us.

Once we got to our grandparents' house, we could race our uncles for a quarter. We would run in the middle of the street, and whoever won would get the money. "On your mark, get set, go!" I would go flying down the street trying to win that quarter, but my brother Ronnie was always faster than me, so he would win every time. It was always so much fun at my grandparents' house. They were the kindest, most loving Louisiana people I have ever known. My grandmother would feed strangers. She would feed everybody and help anybody if she could.

My grandfather was a very smart and educated man who worked for Rockwell Aircraft Company for over fifty years. But I couldn't help but wonder if he and my grandmother even knew how their grandchildren were being treated and neglected not too far away. I'm sure they didn't because our father was very private about what went on in our house, and relatives didn't often visit. He would tell us, "You had better not tell people my business. What happens in this house stays in this house! Do you understand me?" "Yes, Louis," we would answer in unison. We didn't even call our parents Mom or Dad. We called them by their first names, Louis and Gwen. How different is that?

I believe many of our relatives were afraid of my father because he had such a bad temper and was known to get violent at times. They didn't want to make "Brother" mad, so they pretended they did not see anything.

Sandra, Yolanda, and me in Louisiana visiting family – 1975

The party at my grandparents' house started, and everyone was having a great time. There was food, cake, and punch. Most of the adults were drinking, and everyone was giving my father gifts. I got to see all my cousins. But then the fighting began. My father accused one of the old, male family friends of flirting with my mother. My mother explained that was not so, but my father walked up to the man and hit him across the head with the Colt 45 malt liquor bottle. Blood splashed everywhere. As my mother was trying to explain that she and the man were not flirting with each other, my father dragged her by her hair out of the party.

"The party is over. Let's go!" my father shouted. On hearing those words, all five of us children knew we had to run for the door and get into the car because he was mad. We also knew the fighting would continue once we got home. All we could do was go into our room and shut the door as our mother cried and begged him to stop beating her. I developed a hatred for my father. I could never understand why he was so cruel to my mother, beating her so viciously. She seemed to be totally helpless in his hands.

At this time we were really poor, what people call poor-poor, to the point our electricity and gas were turned off, and we were living by candlelight. The kitchen sink and bathroom toilet were stopped up. The plumbing was bad, and my father would make me dip out the days-old water from the kitchen sink and bathroom toilet. It was horrible! I had to take a bucket and dip the poop out of the toilet that had been there for days. I would throw it into the back alley. It was sickening to the point of vomiting and crying at the same time.

The Honey Bucket

It was so bad my siblings and I came up with a name for the bucket. We called it the honey bucket. The honey bucket was actually the poop bucket, but we made humor out of it to help us survive that dehumanizing job. I often looked at my little friends and wondered why they weren't living like I was with no food, lights, or hot water in a house that stank.

My father's health was quickly declining. He had no choice but to go to the hospital. Once he was there, they decided to keep him. One day turned into two days. After a while, it seemed as if he was there for weeks. I was relieved because he had promised my siblings and me a whooping we would never forget. He would say, "It's building up. It's building up!" And we believed him. We lived in so much fear of that day to come, but it never did.

On October 9, 1973, my father died from pneumonia, heart failure, and cirrhosis of the liver. Alcohol addiction killed him at thirty-two years old. He was such a young man. That morning we were all over at our grandparents' house when the phone call came in that "Brother" had passed. All my aunties and uncles, as well as some cousins, were crying, but my emotions were everywhere. The man I had known for thirteen years as my father was gone. I was relieved. My siblings and I were not going to get that whooping he had promised us, and I no longer had to hear or see him brutally beating my mother.

What About Us?

Alcohol addiction destroyed my father's life, and it was continually destroying my mother's as well. I wondered what was going to happen to the five of us and her. I hoped we could live with my grandparents. However, after my father's funeral, my grandmother dropped my mother and all five of us off at our house. The next day when we woke up, our mother was gone. She left. We waited day after day, but still no return of our mother. She had finally found her way of escape. But what about us? We were left alone with no mother or father. My heart was shattered. I couldn't imagine her leaving us at a time we needed her most, but it was true; she was gone.

Our grandmother finally came over to our house to check on us and found out we had been home alone for a week. She gathered some of our things and took us home with her. She called and drove around frantically looking for our mother, but she was nowhere to be found. Different people had told my grandmother they saw my mother partying and living her life. The last hope for our family abandoned us after all our struggles. She was gone. I was thirteen years old. That was a critical age when I needed my mother most.

Many days we sat at my grandmother's house wondering what was going to become of us. Lots of conversations were taking place. What are you going to do with them? Who's going to take care of them? Where is their mother? Where are they going to sleep? We felt so isolated. Caring for five children is a huge responsibility for anyone. Our grandparents had raised their own eight children and were getting older. The way things were done at our house was a lot different from the way they were done at my grandmother's house. We really had no good home training, so we annoyed some of our aunties and uncles who were still living at home with my grandparents.

What are you going to do with them?

Forever Grateful

Thankfully, our grandparents stepped up and our grandmother said she didn't want her grandkids separated. They wanted us all to stay together. She said she would call our paternal grandfather and ask him if he could be of any help. I remember the phone conversation and hearing my grandmother say, "But I don't want to send them to a foster home. I want them all to stay together." She got off the phone and said, "I'm keeping them all together." There was no room for us, but she made room. We slept on the living room floors with blankets and pillows, but she kept us all together. Eventually, she made space for us in her back room, and the five of us slept there together. I will forever be grateful to my grandparents, my father's parents, who stepped up to the plate and took on the responsibility of raising five children.

I was still suffering from my childhood trauma. It was showing up and showing out! I guess the past doesn't always stay in the past. It wasn't until I cried out to the Lord that I got the help I needed. My healing was supernaturally led by the Holy Spirit. He helped me to understand my triggers and how to release the pain by letting it go. The Lord helped me understand I wasn't the trauma I had experienced but a victim of it. He led me through a process of becoming victorious:

1. I had to own it – yes, this is what happened to me.
2. I had to uncover it – from the suppressed place where I hid it.
3. I had to feel it – the pain and emotions by letting it flow.
4. I had to release it – and let it go.

If you or someone you know are suffering from childhood trauma or post-traumatic stress disorder, get help. Pray and ask God to help you with your childhood trauma because, unfortunately, it does not simply go away. It will continue to disrupt your life into adulthood if not dealt with properly. For some, it may require talking to a counselor, therapist, or pastor who will guide them through the process. Simply talk to someone who will listen to your story. This will relieve your burdens and let you express the feelings you suppressed for so many years.

Here are some of the signs of suppressed childhood trauma:

- Depression
- Anger
- Anxiety
- Stress disorder
- Substance abuse
- Alcoholism
- Emotional outbursts
- Problems with relationships
- Difficulty trusting people and more

"For I know the plans I have for you," declares the Lord, "plans to prosper you and not to harm you, plans to give you hope and a future." (Jeremiah 29:11, NIV)

CHAPTER 3

THE SEED WAS PLANTED

Shortly after we went to live with our grandparents, our great-auntie and uncle came to visit us to see how they could help. Auntie Eloise was my grandfather's sister and her husband was Uncle George Richardson. He was the pastor of Bethel Church of God in Christ. I recall them laying hands on us and praying for us, which felt so good. It was as if we were going to be alright. After praying for us, they asked for our clothes and shoe sizes. A few days later when they returned, it felt like Christmas! They had bags and bags of clothes, shoes, books, and toys—so many! We didn't know what to wear first. We were so excited someone loved these five little children with no mother or father. My auntie and uncle were very loving and kind people.

I have always been very proud to be an Elam because of my grandfather, Louis F. Elam Jr., and my great-grandfather, Louis F. Elam Sr., of Violet, Louisiana. They were mighty servants of God. My great-grandfather would travel from Louisiana once a year to visit his children and grandchildren in California. Oh, my, how us great-grandkids would enjoy seeing our Paw-Paw. He would joke around and show us how high he could kick his leg up at eighty and ninety years old. He brought so much joy to our hearts as he jokingly spoke French.

As a little girl, I couldn't figure out what he was saying, but it was funny to me.

At the end of his visit, he would never leave without pulling out that bottle of Pompeian olive oil and anointing us while praying, laying hands, and telling us who we were as the Elam family and God's people. He would also appoint us older kids as the godparents of our younger cousins. This was so funny because we were young teens at this time, and it felt good to be responsible for a goddaughter. "Ronnie and Kathy, you will be the godparents of your cousin Juanyne," he would say. "Look after her and pray for her." So not only is Juanyne my cousin, but she is also the goddaughter of my brother Ronnie and me. We love her.

My aunt Eloise Elam-Richardson, my great-grandfather's daughter and my grandfather's sister, asked my grandparents if she and her husband could pick up my siblings and me for church on Sundays. My grandparents said yes, and Sunday after Sunday, our uncle Elder George Richardson would pick us up, along with our cousins who lived right up the street from my grandparents' house. Bethel Church of God in Christ's ministry bus would faithfully take us to church to learn the Word of God. This was all very new for my siblings and me. We had only been to church one time when our mother took us around the corner from our house to be baptized.

The Invitation

We were invited by some church members walking through the neighborhood encouraging people to come to church. They fed us afterward, but we did not understand what was going on. It felt as if we were just there to eat and get in the water. But at Bethel Church of God in Christ, it was different. We were with family, and the people there actually cared and showed us so much love. This was the first time I had heard the gospel of Jesus Christ. It felt like a breath of fresh air. Finally, someone was ministering to our broken souls. However, it would take a lot of work to change me because I was still full of anger toward my parents and God. How could such a loving God allow me to experience so much pain and tragedy in my life as a child? Yet, Sunday by Sunday, the messages were chipping away at my stony heart.

When my uncle Elder George Richardson preached, he made us feel it deep down in our souls. The saints would cry, shout, dance, and run around the church praising God in the spirit of liberty. It was amazing as my cousin John, who today is a bishop in the Church of God in Christ, would play the drums and my cousin Anthony would be on the organ. No one could beat a tambourine like my cousin Evelyn. There was such a beautiful Spirit of God in this church. After church, they would feed us and take us back home. Being amongst these people was like nothing I had ever experienced. After attending church for a while, one Sunday I accepted Jesus Christ into my heart by faith. I didn't feel any different. Afterward, I went on living my life, but I didn't realize the seed was planted.

Sundays turned into midweek YPWW—Young People's Willing Workers, the training program for youth in my denomination—then choir rehearsals and visits to other churches. Singing songs of praise unto the Lord was the joy of my life. I enjoyed being with my cousins more than anything.

The Seed Was Planted

I was still dealing with the pain of my past. I couldn't understand why my mother would leave her five children when we needed her most. Where was she? Was she OK? Did she think about her children? So many unanswered questions lingered in my mind as I began to pull away from the church. But the seed was already planted by my auntie and uncle.

There is a powerful message in the planting of a seed.

*I have planted, Apollos watered; but God gave the increase.
(1 Corinthians 3:6)*

And he said, so is the kingdom of God, as if a man should cast seed into the ground; and should sleep, and rise night and day, and the seed should spring and grow up, he knoweth not how. For the earth bringeth forth fruit of herself; first the blade, then the ear, after that the full corn in the ear. But when the fruit is brought forth, immediately he putteth in the sickle, because the harvest is come. (Mark 4:26-29)

I love this parable because it teaches us that the gospel seed has power. It teaches us that while we may not always see immediate results, we must remain hopeful for the salvation of family and friends because the gospel will bear fruit in the Lord's timing.

During 1976-1978, I was in high school (David Starr Jordan High). I had also left the church. I wanted to find my own way to see what was out in this big world for me. I felt I was missing out on something with all the church stuff.

High school was amazing. My grandparents had gotten me some of the extra after-school reading help I needed. Now I could spread my wings and enjoy attracting the boys' attention. I did everything I could to maintain it: combing my hair really pretty, as well as keeping my clothes and appearances up.

The messages were chipping away at my stony heart.

I kind of cruised through tenth grade trying to find my way and getting familiar with the school. However, by the time I hit the eleventh and twelfth grades, I was in full bloom. Baby, my hair was always on point. It was time for me to shine. Some of my closest friends were Myra, Penny, Deloris, Denelle, and Dee-Dee, along with my auntie Yolanda and cousin Sandra. We were active young ladies in our high school. From drill team, majorettes, band, track team, ladies club, and student government, we did it all and had a ball!

**With my school friends in front of David Starr Jordan High – 1978
l-r: me, Penny, Deloris, Myra, Yolanda**

I joined everything I could on campus. I even tried gymnastics until I sprained my ankle. Twelfth grade, bam! I won the most popular girl title in my senior year! Yes, me, lil-ol' skinny Kathy Elam. I think out of all the different groups, clubs, and sports I was involved in on campus, I enjoyed running track the most. Our track team at Jordan High was the best in those days, and our track coaches, Ms. Dezen and Coach Washington, were the best coaches ever. They actually cared about us students and our future.

Aka Dee-Dee

This is where I grew close to one of the most beautiful young ladies you could have ever known—Florence Griffith. We called her Dee-Dee. For the first time in high school, I had someone I could share my most personal secrets and dreams with. She would give me the best positive advice. We were friends. We would always play around

Dee-Dee and me at David Starr Jordan High School in the girls' locker room practicing our splits – 1977

in the girls' locker room trying to get cute before we went out on the track to practice. That's where all the cute football players and track and field athletes would be, and they were looking at us. We would file our teeth straight and put baby powder under our eyebrows as eye shadow; we always loved beauty tips. We had so much fun at practice and in the girls' locker room seeing who could really get their split down. Dee-Dee could always do a split and make it look easy.

I got to see who Dee-Dee was close-up as a young lady. She was as beautiful inside as she was outside. We would have track meets on the weekends and sometimes the city or state meets. We would all spend the night over at our coach Ms. Dezen's house. She would take all of us young girls shopping for food. Whatever we needed, she would provide. Oftentimes I couldn't afford certain necessities, but she would always take care of them for me. I'm still grateful to her.

Dee-Dee was setting records in the 100-yard dash while we were still in high school. I ran with her on the Jordan High School girls' track team. We both also tried gymnastics, the drill team, and majorettes together. We loved twirling our batons at the football games. But the homecoming parades were the best as we wore the shiny costumes that Ms. Hall and Pam designed for us. The Halls would teach us how to spin our batons. Sometimes Dee-Dee and I would practice at my grandparents' house just to be extra perfect. Dee-Dee was a perfectionist, and by the time the parade started, we were ready to strut our stuff down 103rd Street in Jordan High's homecoming parade. Dee-Dee was so full of life. To know her was to love her.

We were all just a bunch of young girls with dreams and goals. After high school Dee-Dee and I took two different paths in life. She continued pursuing her track and field career and I went on a journey in search of my mother which took me down a deep, dark path of prostitution, drugs and nearly losing my life.

Me graduating from
David Starr Jordan High – 1978

We were all young girls with dreams and goals.

Years later, on a number of occasions, family members and friends would tell me how Dee-Dee would ask about me and reach out to me. But I was in a state of shame and embarrassment. How could I have let myself fall so far from the goals and dreams I once shared in conversations with Dee-Dee as we walked around Jordan High School's track field. I didn't want her to know about the choices I made, however she may have known because the streets talk!

After we graduated high school, Dee-Dee continued her track and field journey, which took her to the Olympics. When my family shared the news with me that she had made it to the Olympics, I was not surprised. I always knew greatness was in her. Tears of joy ran down my face. My friend had won the gold medal at the Olympics for the U.S. She was Flo-Jo to the world, Florence Griffith Joyner; to those of us close to her, she was always Dee-Dee because her middle name was Delorez. We were just girls from the ghetto with big dreams and goals.

After high school, I was still haunted by abandonment and the emptiness of my mother's absence. I was interested in nursing, so I began taking some classes at Southwest College, later Compton College, and doing some internship at Martin Luther King Hospital. At the same time, I was working at the American-Indian free clinic on Long Beach Boulevard as a nurse assistant to make some money. I was doing a lot but ultimately trying to find just what I really loved doing. I even tried modeling.

Dee-Dee winning the gold medal at the 1988 Seoul Olympics

A Piece of the Puzzle

Someone told me my mother was living in San Bernardino. The person gave me a number where she could be contacted. At first I resisted calling her. I figured, why should I? She should have been the one contacting me. She was the one who ran off and abandoned her five children. Why should we call her? But inside I was so excited to know she was alive.

I really wanted to hear her voice, so my grandmother said we were going to call her. All five of us were in the living room with our ears near the phone as my grandmother called. She asked to speak to Gwen.

My mother said, "This is Gwen. Who is calling?"

My grandmother said, "This is Mrs. Elam. I have your children close to the phone."

We could hear our mother crying, saying, "Oh, my God, my kids are on the phone." She said, "I'm so sorry." We cried too. She asked our ages and even remembered our names and specific things we liked to do. She promised to visit us, but she never did. Later she told me she was just too ashamed.

I got her address and had a friend drive me to San Bernardino to see her. I just wanted to physically look at her to make sure she was well. I guess I was trying to understand what would keep a mother from her children for all these years. It was a piece of the puzzle I just had to find. I found her living with a family in San Bernardino and her new boyfriend, Nathan, who was actually pretty cool. When I first knocked on the door, he answered, "Who is it?"

I replied, "Kathy, can I speak to Gwen?"

He opened the door and said, "Gwen, it's your daughter Kathy."

My mother ran from the back screaming and hollering, "Oh, my God! Kathy!" She hugged me tightly as she cried. I introduced my friend who had come with me because he really wanted me to find my mother. I didn't bring my other sisters and brothers because I didn't know what to expect. This was something I needed to do alone because, as the oldest girl, it was hard trying to survive without my mother. A mother can teach her daughter many personal things about herself. That's what I longed for.

Today my relationship with all my children is good, but especially my daughters Kierra and Kamerra, my K-Girls. I taught them their value at a young age because many young and older women lack identity. My grandmother and grandfather did their best, and I will forever be grateful. I wouldn't be the woman I am today without their love, support, guidance, and prayers. But at times their hands were full, so I had to just learn from the school of hard knocks on the streets.

My mother was trying to make up for lost time, but I was almost nineteen years old, working, going to college, and taking care of myself. She was still drinking, but at least the physical abuse was over for her. Nathan really loved my mother and was very good to her. However, the strangest thing was, she would fight him like my father used to fight her. That was crazy!

Nathan's Baby Brother

She asked me to visit again, and I said yes, and yes, and yes. I was even more interested when I met Nathan's baby brother, a handsome guy with his eyes on me. We fell in love, and the visits to San Bernardino became more and more frequent. I left all the goals and dreams I was pursuing in Los Angeles behind.

After about a year, Nathan's brother and I got married. I was pregnant with my first baby girl. She was born on December 7, 1980—

Kuleshia Star, one of the most beautiful babies I had ever seen in my life. I don't call her beautiful just because she was mine. She was simply gorgeous.

One year later, I was pregnant again. This time it was a handsome baby boy named Anthony Derek Jones Jr. Wow! I was married, had two kids, and was living in San Bernardino. I had left Watts and was living this new life close to my mother.

After a while, our marriage became abusive. The fighting and drinking had taken its toll. I found myself running down the street in my negligee from my drunk husband. But, unlike my mother, I was not going to stay in an abusive relationship. It was time for me to leave. I gathered my two children and headed back to Los Angeles. "Love doesn't live here anymore." I filed for a divorce, but to my surprise I discovered we were never legally married. We never filed the paperwork from the minister. My lawyer said, "I guess you don't need me anymore because you are not married!" Oh, well, we were young and inexperienced with two beautiful children, but it was over.

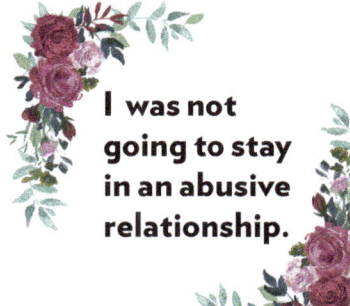

I was not going to stay in an abusive relationship.

The drinking and fighting were too much. I saw it coming. I knew one of us would end up getting hurt really badly if I didn't leave. I was not my mother. I fought back. If you hit me, you were going to get hit back or shot! "Tit-for-tat is a fair game" was my philosophy back in those days.

Untreated Trauma

I was so full of anger and rage from my untreated childhood trauma while my "I thought husband" was knocking on its door. Dealing with childhood trauma, anger, and rage as an adult is one of the worst ordeals. If it's not correctly addressed, you will channel it the wrong way. It has a way of being suppressed in our subconscious for years like a pressure cooker waiting to explode. Anger is a powerful emotion. It can cause you to hurt other people and destroy yourself if left untreated. Therefore, the next time you get so enraged you feel as if you are going to lose control, stop for a second and ask yourself: where is this coming from? Then you'll find your triggers.

I am so glad I got out of that toxic, dangerous relationship. We were both full of childhood pain—a disaster waiting to happen.

If you are filled with anger, seek help. Studies show that one out of five Americans has an anger management problem. Never allow anger to rule your life. You rule your anger; otherwise, it can become a tremendous obstacle. Don't hold grudges; they will hold back your personal growth.

Be ye angry, and sin not: let not the sun go down upon your wrath. (Ephesians 4:26)

CHAPTER 4

WHO AM I BECOMING?

By the time I moved back to Watts, things had changed. It was the '80s and some of my old neighborhood friends who were walking when I left were now driving Mercedes-Benz and Rolls-Royce vehicles. They were draped in gold rope chains and living the life of the rich and famous. It was as if someone had busted a piñata full of money over South-Central. I asked my oldest brother what this was all about. He said that's how they were doing it now in Watts and pulled out a large stack of money. I was shocked. When I left Watts, my brother was painting cars and cutting out lowriders. Now he owned Cadillacs, Mercedes, Corvettes, BMWs, and classic cars. I knew painting neighborhood cars would not get him all that money.

Drugs had flooded our community. People who were once very influential and hardworking were addicted to crack-cocaine. Overnight they lost everything. Many signed over their cars and deeds to their homes just to get a high. Several beautiful girls I knew from back in the day were now addicted to crack-cocaine as well. They were doing any and everything to get that high. Someone gave them the street name "Strawberries" meaning they would do anything sexual to get high. Crackheads were males and females who would steal anything that wasn't bolted down. This included family members' money, jewelry, etc. They would sell things to chase that next high. But all the crackheads weren't poor and needy. Some were very wealthy. Even celebrities would come down to Watts and Compton to buy crack-cocaine.

All this turmoil and these lavish lifestyles came at a very high price. Both drug dealers and crackheads were being found dead in back alleys and in the trunks of cars. Many were tied up in their homes and had their bodies mutilated, shot down at the corner while standing on their street, and several others were set-up by their own homeboys they grew up with. The '80s were crazy. We were living a mafia lifestyle on the streets of South-Central with gangs and drug dealers everywhere. Nowhere was safe.

A Full-Course Meal

I knew many of the guys and girls who had died; some went to high school with me. It broke my heart. They were some really good guys and young ladies just trying to survive the ghetto life. Did the struggle make it right to sell drugs? No, but the mentality at that time was you cannot put a full-course meal in front of a hungry person, walk away, and tell him not to eat it. As soon as you turn your back, that person will grab the plate of food and eat! Someone was putting a full-course meal in front of us in South-Central and saying, "I'm walking away, but don't eat it." Not everyone was strong enough to ignore the plate of food.

I didn't know the game, and my big brother wasn't trying to teach me. Later he explained that wasn't the road he wanted me to go down. But I was still trying to figure out what everybody was doing to make this kind of money and rolling so lavishly. I got together with a couple of old associates to party, and they introduced me to crack-cocaine. They told me it was the drug everyone was using at the time and made it seem really cool. They asked if I wanted to try it. And I did. After all, my life was headed downhill anyway. Maybe I could numb some of the pain from my past. Childhood trauma was still haunting me, along with a failed marriage. "So let's get high," I said.

My life changed drastically. I spiraled downward faster than I had expected. I was doing things I never thought I would. Like many people who make some of the same choices, as I child, I had been handled inappropriately. That was definitely a factor. When the innocence and self-worth of a child is taken away, they become open to all kinds of abuse and destructive behavior.

You see, anytime you don't have direction and purpose for your life, the devil will give you one—like the prostitution he gave me. I hooked up with my old homegirl who was now a prostitute going by the name of Bonnie. She was making lots of money from prostitution. I joined her, and we became outlaws making money. We answered to no one and collected our own cash. She had my back, and I had hers. But at the end of the day, prostitution left me feeling empty and degraded; shame flooded my soul.

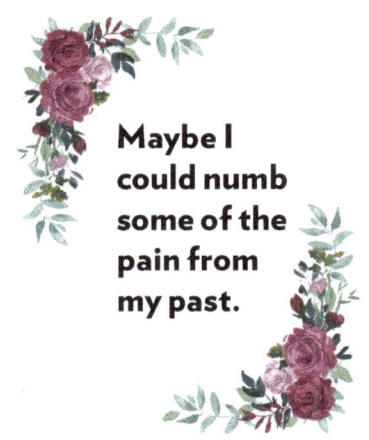

Maybe I could numb some of the pain from my past.

Prostitution is very dehumanizing. Most prostitutes are big drug users or alcoholics trying to numb the inner pain and shame. No amount of money is worth the pain a woman experiences from prostitution. If you or someone you know is locked into this type of lifestyle, try to get help. Most of all, pray for the person because prostitution is darkness at its worst. I used drugs to sedate my emotional and psychological pain.

The Inheritance

I saw the characteristics of my parents in me, the very ones I detested: anger and a bad temper. I seemed to have inherited them. It did not take much for me to physically fight. Truth is I was in pain screaming out for help, but no one could hear me. I looked good on the outside but was tormented inside. My life had become a repeated cycle of the dysfunctional behavior I saw growing up.

I took pleasure in dominating men and taking their money. I was never loyal to any of them. I enjoyed watching them beg me to be with them as I took their money and played games. However, unlike my parents, I always made sure my two children were well taken care of and in a safe environment with my sisters Toni or Cynthia or their grandmother Bertha. My children were always with family who loved them. I never wanted them to experience what I did. I spent most of my money on my kids, dressed them well, and gave them the best to eat. But it all came at the price of their mother's pain.

No one in my family knew what I was doing and that I was making money through prostitution. I had lost my way big-time. My childhood pain had now caught up with me. After all, the first man in my life slapped me down at a young age. I was acting out in the strangest ways.

A Ticking Time Bomb

I recall getting into a car with one guy to turn a trick. His car had suicide doors where you could get in, but you couldn't get out. No handles were on the passenger doors to get out. Once I got into the car, he began to put on some black leather gloves and told me, "I'm going to kill you." At that point, I thought to myself, does he really think I'm going to just sit here and let him kill me!?! I started kicking, screaming, fighting, biting, scratching, and beating him until the car drove out of control. He had no choice but to hit the lock and let this crazy girl from Watts out of his car. I staggered out like Tina Turner in the *What's Love Got to Do with It* movie after she and Ike had been fighting. What the trick didn't know was that I was full of anger and rage from my childhood, and he was about to be my outlet. I wanted to say, "Stop playing, man! I'm a ticking time bomb ready to explode."

Does he think I'm going to sit here and let him kill me!?!

I began drinking lots of alcohol and using drugs day and night—uppers to keep me up and downers to help me sleep. I was trying to self-medicate the pain I was suffering. One time I got so high on drugs I had to be rushed to the hospital. I had mixed multiple drugs together and blacked out. An associate got me to the hospital just in time for them to help me come down from a drug overdose. It looked as if that episode would have stopped me, but it didn't. The pain from my past was too severe. It's amazing how we can look so good on the outside but be tormented on the inside.

"Let's go"

I recall being in a drug house getting high when all of a sudden someone tapped me on the shoulder and said, "Let's go." I looked back to see who it was that was talking to me, but no one was there. I continued to get high, but someone tapped me again and said, "Let's go!" with a stronger voice than before. I got up, put the drugs down, walked out of the drug house, and never went back. Later, after giving my life to the Lord, His Spirit revealed that the devil had a plan to kill me that night because he comes to steal, kill, and destroy. But God sent His angel to rescue me because I had not yet met my destiny.

My oldest brother Ronnie found out I was on drugs. He was very mad at me as the two of us have always shared a very special bond—more like twins—only a year apart. We struggled as the oldest two and oftentimes had to hold things together for our siblings while we were just kids ourselves. He told me, "Kathy, I didn't want you doing what I did. That's why I wouldn't tell you about it. But, Sis, drugs are not to be used in this game. They are to be sold. I had better not ever hear of you using drugs again."

From that point, the game changed for me. We became like Bonnie and Clyde. He bought me a new Cadillac Seville that was black on black. It had a bumper kit with gold leafing around it sitting on rims.

Sister and brother bond.
Me visiting Ronnie in prison – 1989

He made sure my children and I were taken care of and kept a close watch on me until I kicked the drugs. However, he still didn't know about the prostitution. I hid it from all my family members. Shortly after, I stopped that as well. From that point on, I became a drug dealer. I never used drugs again, cold turkey. I stopped, but I picked up the habit of cigarettes and continued to drink alcohol. It was all about getting my money in and out of town because I needed to get my children their own home.

My grandfather also found out I was using drugs and had a very long talk with me. He said he and my grandmother were praying for me because they knew I was in pain from my childhood. They believed God was going to heal me. I listened out of respect, but I really wasn't ready for the God thing again. After all, where was God when my mother was being beaten beyond recognition by the man who was my father and their son? I love and respect my grandparents dearly. So I assured them I was off drugs, but I didn't tell them I was dealing them.

Me in the drug life – 1985

Ghetto Fabulous

I was high rolling ghetto style. I say ghetto style because a couple of hundred thousand was all you needed to be rolling ghetto style. We had the game locked in. No more broke days for us. No more picking up scrap on the train tracks, no more eating green peaches and looking for food in trash cans. If you've ever been hungry and starving, you never want to do that again. It is an indescribable pain. From state to state, my brother and I traveled and collected money.

We became like Bonnie and Clyde.

In the crazy '80s, lots of guys and girls in the ghetto were making big money. Those of us who had it hard growing up felt it was our way out—or so we thought! Many of us owned and drove very expensive cars and wore lots of gold chains with diamonds. Many bought beautiful homes and opened businesses. We were always fly wearing Louis Vuitton, Gucci, Fendi, Prada, Fila, Nike, Adidas, etc. I often laugh today when my children think most of these designers' styles are new to me. I tell them everything goes around and comes full circle.

I stayed as we would say "fly" from top to bottom. Most of my homegirls were fly as well because it was all about living the life and having fun doing it. We would all meet up at the skating rinks: World on Wheels and Skate Depot. All the skaters would be on the floor rolling around the rink to "Hey, Love" by Stevie Wonder. Who can forget Oldies but Goodies night? Then there were the Friday night street races.

On Saturdays, all lowriders met up to caravan with the drop-tops. The fly girls would be sitting in the middle with our feathered hairstyles bouncing while our dudes would be hitting the switch all the way to picnics, concerts, clubs, or whatever hangout was happening. As fly girls, we kept our hair on point. Having basket-weave braids was the look. My favorite hairstylist was my sister Toni; no one could braid hair like her. Mantrap was the nail shop on Crenshaw to get your nails and feet hooked up.

In our hood, one fly girl recognized another fly girl because all our dudes were high rollers with big money. Once a year, some of the high rollers would throw a big-player ball party. My brother Ronnie and a lot of other high rollers and homies would pull up in Mercedes-Benz, Lamborghini, Ferrari, Rolls-Royce, and some of the fly lowrider classic cars, not rented but owned.

I was living the life shopping on Rodeo Drive in Beverly Hills and wearing top designer clothes. My dude was also a high roller taking very good care of me. He took me from driving a Cadillac Seville to sporting a Jaguar. The house on Anzac was the headquarters where we all met. Everybody knew the quarters was the hangout for lots of fly girls and gangsters to party and drink.

I thought the relationship I had with my new high roller Boo would work out because we spent lots of time together. Plus, we were pretty much into the same game of drug dealing and the street life. But, to my surprise, I found out he was married. Wow! I had been with this married man for a couple of months. I thought married men were supposed to go home at night. How could he be married yet spend so much time with me? He even helped me get the money I needed to move into my house.

Me with my basket-weave braids and in the life – 1987

Me at the Players' Ball in white mink – 1987

WHO AM I BECOMING?

Me and my homegirls Tammy, Juanita, Angie (RIP), Toni my sister, Ann and Deloris 1986

The day the truth was revealed, we were on our way to the summer fest concert. Dressed alike from head to toe, we were rolling down Wilmington on our way to hit the 91 Freeway in one of his many luxury cars. Out of the blue, a woman driving behind us in one of his other cars started blowing the horn constantly. I asked him who was in his car blowing us down. He wouldn't say. He only pulled over and asked me to stay in the car, not to get out. All I know is he was cussing this woman out, but I couldn't hear the exact conversation. He returned to the car, pulled off, and continued to the concert. Again, I asked who she was and why she was so upset. He said, "I'll tell you later. It's a long story." I fell for it! My morals and values were all out the window, and I fell for the lies. I stayed in the relationship in spite of my instinct to leave. At the end of the day, I lacked nothing. He took great care of me. But not all money is good money!

"Who am I becoming?"

The Spot in Compton

It was time to get a home for my children. My boyfriend went to jail on some drugs and gun charges, and I thought that was the opportunity to leave, but it was hard. My heart was caught up in this mess I had allowed. At the same time, I had a drug spot in Compton. So I made arrangements with my children's father's mother, Bertha, who was a beautiful, kind, and loving grandmother, to keep my kids for one year. That way I could get enough money to buy them a house. She said yes. Every weekend I would visit them, pick them up, take them out to eat, shop, and spend time with them. However, during the week, it was all about getting my money to give my children a home.

One night I decided to make lasagna at one of the drug spots and hang out. I called over some friends as I always loved sharing food and helping people who were less fortunate than me. Many times I would help people get back on their feet because I didn't want to see them on the street. But this particular night we were drinking, partying, playing cards, and listening to oldies—simply having a good time. I didn't want to pass up any money, so I was still selling drugs at the spot.

I had a slit in the screen bar door and was pushing it in and out so I wouldn't miss any money! I had to get my kids a house and nothing was going to stop me. My high roller man was in jail and the money had stopped. So I had to get it moving again even in the midst of all the danger associated with the neighborhood on Sloan Street. That area was full of drug dealers and gangbangers. Every night, gunshots permeated the night.

One night, at about 2:00 AM, gunshots began to go off. As I hit the floor, I could see bullet holes coming through my walls. All I could do was lie there on the floor until the shooting stopped. After a few minutes, I heard someone hollering from outside "Call the ambulance! Call 911!" So I walked out my door to see what happened. I was shocked to see five young men from the neighborhood shot down and fighting for their lives. It was said that they had been hanging out when some guys from another neighborhood came and did a drive-by. It broke my heart as I watched the bodies of these young men gasping for air as their blood ran out into the streets they once played on.

Me with my son Anthony Jr. and his grandmother "Bertha Mae" (RIP). She was beautiful inside and out – 1985

I could hear the sirens of the ambulance as a lot of us were out there trying to stop the bleeding and shouting "Hold on! Help is coming!" Once the ambulance arrived, the first responders worked frantically to save their lives. But, one by one, they began to cover those boys with white sheets as they waited for the coroner to arrive.

I returned to my spot with tears running down my face and thinking to myself, "Who am I becoming?" I had to question myself as I looked at the bullet holes in the kitchen and bedroom. Still, days later I was in the spot again, partying with some friends and drinking.

Just as I was putting the lasagna in the oven, something hit the front door. It sounded as if a bomb had gone off. Everyone was stunned and wondering, "What was that?" When it hit again, I ran to get my gun as someone shouted, "It's *one time*!" That was code for the police. I then broke and ran to my stash, grabbed the drugs, and rushed to the bathroom to flush them down the toilet… but it was too late. The police had turned the water off before they raided me. I ran out of the restroom trying to get to the kitchen to flush the drugs down the sink's garbage disposal, but before I could get there, they broke through the front door and said, "Police! Don't move!"

As I looked down the barrel of a .45 revolver, I threw my hands up. The police said, "Get down on the ground and keep your hands behind your head!" They handcuffed me on the floor. I had sold to an undercover cop, and now I was going to jail. Just before they took me out of the house, one of the black female officers asked me, "Can I have that oldie tape you're playing?" Back in those days, we had cassette tapes. All I played were oldies. I still recall what was playing that night as I was being hauled off to jail: "You Beat Me to the Punch" by Mary Wells. And I guess they did!

"Yes, you can," I replied. I knew I wouldn't be listening to oldies for a while.

CHAPTER 5

IF YOU GET ME OUT OF THIS ONE

"Let everyone in here go," I told the police. "They have nothing to do with any of this!" I was being taken down to Compton police station. They booked me, and I spent the night in a cold cell, while my brother Ronnie tried to bail me out but couldn't. There was an old prostitution case that had not been resolved, and it turned into a warrant. The next day, I was taken downtown LA behind the men's prison until they transferred me to Sybil Brand women's prison.

I was stuck for a few months fighting two cases. That gave me time to think about what I was doing with my life and where I was headed. I remember saying to God, whom I hadn't spoken to in years, "If You get me out of this, I'll do the right thing from here out." But that was just jailhouse drama talk. God saw right through it and knew I was still my biggest enemy.

I knew my children were expecting to see me on the weekend as usual. Wow! And I had just about enough money to get them a home with their own rooms. During this time, I had to go back and forth to court often. I received visits from my family members. On one visit, they brought my two children to see me, which was the hardest thing for me. I told my family, "Please, don't bring my children back up here again. I can't handle it, and this is not the image of their mother I want them to remember."

BROKEN BEYOND RECOGNITION

A couple of months later, I was released from Sybil Brand prison Dorm 5000 with a lot of instructions that I didn't comply with. Talk about cycles. I was going around in many cycles that I didn't know how to break. Once again, as soon as I got out of jail, I tried to make enough money to buy my children a home where we could all be together. I didn't have much time because I had asked their grandmother to give me one year. I only had about three months left. Finally, I got the money I needed to get my children a home! I was so excited. I went and got my two kids from San Bernardino, thanked their grandmother, gave her lots of money, and headed back to LA. I got a call that the house wouldn't be available for a couple of months, so I decided to temporarily rent an apartment on Avalon and Century in Los Angeles.

Kuleshia and Anthony Jr. on Big Wheels – 1985

My daughter Kuleshia was in kindergarten. I used my grandmother's address on 113th and Wilmington so she could attend my old elementary school. Anthony was too young for school.

That was one of the happiest days of my life.

While I was preparing to move into our new home in Inglewood, I temporarily enrolled Kuleshia in school. Then it happened. We moved into our new home in Inglewood. Yes! My children had their own beds and rooms. That was one of the happiest days of my life. The three of us were so excited. I took them shopping. I got them new clothes and toys, and anything they wanted, they had. We decorated. I was so glad to have them back with me. I went and got my niece Melanesha, aka NeNe, my sister Toni's daughter. Melanesha was a very close cousin to my children along with my friend Myrna and her daughter Veronique. In fact, Veronique was Kuleshia's best friend.

The Catch-Up Mission

On the weekends, we would all get together and go to Magic Mountain, Disneyland, Sea World, or Knoxberry Farm. It was as if I was on a catch-up mission to do all the things I wanted to do with them. Every weekend we did something fun. We would go

Kuleshia and Anthony at Chuck E. Cheese playing in balls – 1985

somewhere to celebrate our reunion. My focus was on making my children totally happy. People would often say, "Kathy, you spoil your children." And I would say, "I just want them to have everything I didn't have."

Me and Kuleshia on a moped celerbrating her 5th birthday – 1985

Kuleshia and Anthony Jr. on Easter – 1985

It was around Halloween. My daughter Kuleshia's elementary school was having a Halloween contest. I dressed her like a little maid and her little brother an old man. We had so much family fun taking pictures. Afterward, we went out to dinner to celebrate that Kuleshia had won the contest! She was enjoying her elementary school, so I didn't want to remove her in the middle of the semester. I was waiting for the semester to end to transfer her to her new school.

Kuleshia being presented as the winner of the Halloween contest at school by the school staff – 1986

CHAPTER 6

I CAN'T BREATHE

A couple of weeks later, Kuleshia came home from school complaining that her head was hurting. I asked her if she had fallen at school, and she said no. I said, "OK, go lie down for a little while; maybe you played too hard at school today." She did what I said, but as I was preparing her for bed later on that evening, she was still complaining about her head. I took her to the hospital to find out what was going on. The doctor diagnosed her with the flu, prescribed some antibiotics, and said, "Keep her home from school for a few days." He sent us home.

I kept her out of school the next day and was giving her the medication, along with children's Tylenol® because a fever had started to develop. I figured in a few days, it was going to pass and everything was going to be alright. She just had a bad cold.

At the same time, my goddaughter LaNette was living with me. She was a teenager, so I asked her to keep an eye on Kuleshia while she was resting. I had to make a run. Not long after, my youngest brother Papa stopped by my house to visit, but I wasn't there. He and LaNette called me in panic and said, "Kathy, you need to come back. Kuleshia is really hot and shaking." I rushed back.

As Papa said, Kuleshia was unresponsive and very hot. Immediately, I put her into the car and had a friend of mine drive as I held her and repeatedly called her name, "Kuleshia! Kuleshia!" Her eyes were rolling back in her head and her body was burning. All kinds of thoughts were racing through my mind. I figured it was more than the flu; maybe she was choking on something and as soon as we got to the hospital, everything would be alright.

My friend was driving extremely fast, running through red lights and all, until we were pulled over by the police for speeding. He stopped, and the police officers approached the car with their guns drawn saying, "Put your hands up! Let me see your hands!" I shouted to the police officer, "My daughter is not responding, and we're trying to get her to the hospital. Please, let us go!" They opened the car door and saw I was telling the truth. They transferred Kuleshia and me to the back of the police car with their sirens on and told my friend to follow but slow it down. They rushed us to the nearest hospital. Immediately, they took her to the back of the hospital and ran tests after tests. They were moving very quickly with her and asked me several questions about what happened.

I told them when she came home from school, she was complaining about a headache, so I took her to the hospital where they diagnosed her with the flu and gave her medication. I asked them to let me see my daughter. The nurse said, "You will get to see her, but right now they need information from you for the doctors." She said they were attending to my daughter, and she would be alright.

Something Didn't Feel Right
I was freaking out. What was wrong with my child? I was crying because something didn't feel right. They asked me to sign papers for special tests to be done. A specific test involved pulling fluid off her spine. I finally got to her after what seemed to be hours. But actually it was just a few minutes. She was lying there looking sleepy. I ran, kissed her, and began talking to her. After about an hour had passed, the doctor came into the room. Immediately, I

stood up expecting some good news. But he said, "Your daughter is in a coma."

"Coma! No!" I screamed and hit the floor on my knees. Everything I knew about a coma was not good.

I was crying hysterically and began to feel helpless. I asked the doctors what was next. They said more test results were pending. They had tested the fluid on her spine, but the results were not back yet. They promised to let me know their findings as soon as they got them. My daughter's father was notified, and he was on his way from San Bernardino to Los Angeles.

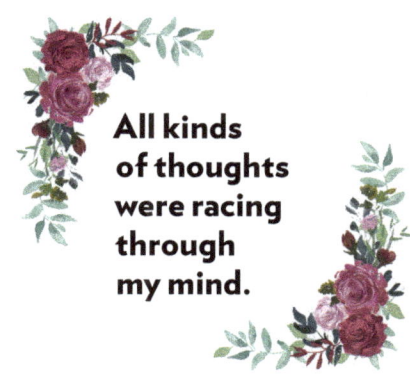

All kinds of thoughts were racing through my mind.

"You might want to pray"

About two hours later, the doctors came into the room again. This time they said Kuleshia had meningococcal meningitis, a rare but serious bacterial infection of the membranes surrounding the brain and spinal cord. They said the area was full of bacteria so the fluid that should be clear was in a milky state; hence, she was in a coma. We were told those who survive this illness were left with disabilities such as deafness, brain damage, and neurological disabilities. The bacteria had traveled to her brain. They were treating her with very strong antibiotics while monitoring her closely. They said we might want to pray.

I cried hysterically with everything in me. I stayed at the hospital day and night as the days went by. I held her hands and talked to her as she continued to be unresponsive in the coma. The next few days, she had to be placed on a life support system to keep her breathing as her body was becoming weaker. I talked to her continually because I always felt she would wake up. It was just a matter of time, I thought. We would get through this. She was going to wake up and everything would be alright; we could continue our fantastic weekends.

All my family and friends were there with many encouraging words. But I wanted to take the doctor up on those last words, "You might want to pray." Where would I begin? I thought prayer was something you did in church and just on Sundays. Nevertheless, I went down to the chapel in the hospital, got on my knees, and prayed an empty prayer. I was so far away from God, and it seemed He was so far away from me. I was lost and hadn't been to church since my early days at Bethel Church of God in Christ with my auntie and uncle. Now I was pleading and begging God not to take my daughter from me. "Take me," I said. "She's just a little girl, please!" I lay on the altar in the hospital chapel for hours crying until my family came and got me.

A week after Kuleshia was hospitalized, the doctor said they wanted to run one last test on her brain called a CT scan to check the brainwaves. It would tell if her brain was still active. They said the test would be done the following morning. I went back to the room, sat next to my daughter, put my finger in her hand, and talked to her. I told her how much I needed her, how much I loved her, and how I couldn't live without her. I felt a gentle squeeze on my finger. "Yes," I said. "She can hear me." The doctors came in again and checked her pupil dilation, as well as her vital signs. They said, "No, she's still the same." But I knew what I felt; was she saying goodbye?

The next day, they ran the last test on her brain. They called her father, our family, and me to come into the conference room of the hospital. We got the most devastating news I have ever heard in my life. My daughter's brain was dead; there was no brain activity at all. The doctors explained that her vital signs had failed and the breathing we saw was only the support of the breathing machine. Her body had already started decomposing.

An Impossible Decision

They asked us if we wanted them to take her off the life support machine. How do you ask a mother or father to make that kind of decision? We had to instruct them to end my baby's suffering. I felt lifeless. I couldn't breathe. Kuleshia's father and I hugged each other and cried.

Our baby girl was gone, and we had a huge decision to make. In anguish, her father hit the glass window in the hospital and cut his hand badly. Blood was gushing from it. I remember running down the hall of the hospital into my daughter's room screaming, crying, and begging God not to let her die. I grabbed her lifeless body, trying to take her home. I was broken and could not let her go. It brought back the pain of my mother's separation from me as a child and that feeling of abandonment. It felt as if I was leaving my baby. I just couldn't!

My firstborn child, who had given me a purpose to live, was gone. I grabbed her in the bed as the nurses struggled to get me to let go of her. I had to be sedated at the hospital because the pain was more than I could bear. I couldn't breathe. I didn't want to breathe!

How could this be? My Kuleshia Starr Jones was gone. I had worked so hard to give her everything I didn't have. Maybe not the way I should have gotten it, but everything I did was for my children. I sacrificed and put up with so much. I did things I didn't want to do just to get the money I needed to give my children a better life and home—and now this! She lay there

I had worked so hard to give her everything I didn't have.

just as beautiful as a little angel but lifeless. I was very angry with God. I didn't understand why or how He could allow this to happen.

Leaving the hospital, I wanted to die; the pain was unbearable. My siblings and family members were all broken in tears. We could not understand what had happened.

Days later, the health department called me and explained that all my family and friends who had been in contact with my daughter would have to be vaccinated because the bacteria were highly contagious. One of the nurses who had cared for my daughter contracted the virus and had passed away as well. That caused even deeper pain as I hurt for her family also. I panicked because my baby boy, Anthony Jr., and my niece might have had it as well. They were the closest to her. We all went down to the health department to be vaccinated and tested. All the tests came back negative. Everyone was fine. But my little son Anthony Jr. (Truck) had lost his big sister, and I had lost my beautiful daughter. So many people were hurt by her death.

My little angel was only five years old. She died just a few weeks before her birthday. She never made it to her sixth year. The pain of losing a child is indescribable. It felt as if my heart had been ripped out of my body. I didn't know what the days were. I didn't know what time it was. My whole world came to a halt, and I asked God why I was here. I have suffered so much in my life. I have known pain even from a child, but nothing compares to the loss of my child. Kuleshia was dead.

A few days later, her elementary school found out what happened and called me with their condolences. They said my daughter might have contracted the virus from a little girl in her classroom. The little girl in my daughter's class was diagnosed with meningitis and taken out of the school. I asked why all the parents weren't notified.

The principal stated an alert was sent out to all parents. However, many of us never got it.

It was time to make funeral arrangements, which was the hardest thing I have ever had to do. I was so thankful for my siblings, Ronnie, Toni, Cynthia, and Louis (Papa), along with my grandparents, who were all right by my side. My aunties, uncles, cousins, and lots of family friends all helped me through this tragedy that was meant to kill me. Looking back now, I feel impressed to share this with anyone who has lost a child or a loved one: don't give up! As much as it feels like you can't take another breath, you can! Relax and breathe. Better days are coming. Surround yourself with people of faith who will speak life into you. These people are very important as they will live for you and believe for you until you can for yourself. You. Can. Make. It!

Me with family support l-r Tammy, Toni, Yolanda, and Cynthia – 1986

70 BROKEN BEYOND RECOGNITION

Pallbearers Melvin, Michael, Ronnie, Louis (Papa), Warren, and Eddie

My brother Ronnie who I am forever grateful to

Pink and White

I remember telling everyone in my family I didn't want my little princess's funeral to be dark and black because she was a little girl who loved life. So we made it look like a wedding: pink and white. At that time, those were not popular colors for men to wear, but the pallbearers each wore pink and white for my daughter. I really appreciated it all. These were hard-core guys who put down their gangster hand that day for my daughter and wore pink and white. My oldest brother Ronnie paid for everything, and I'm forever grateful for him. "Just tell me what you want, Sis, and I'll make it happen." And he did.

At the funeral, I felt empty. As I knelt beside her casket at the gravesite, someone took this picture.

Me kneeling at the casket

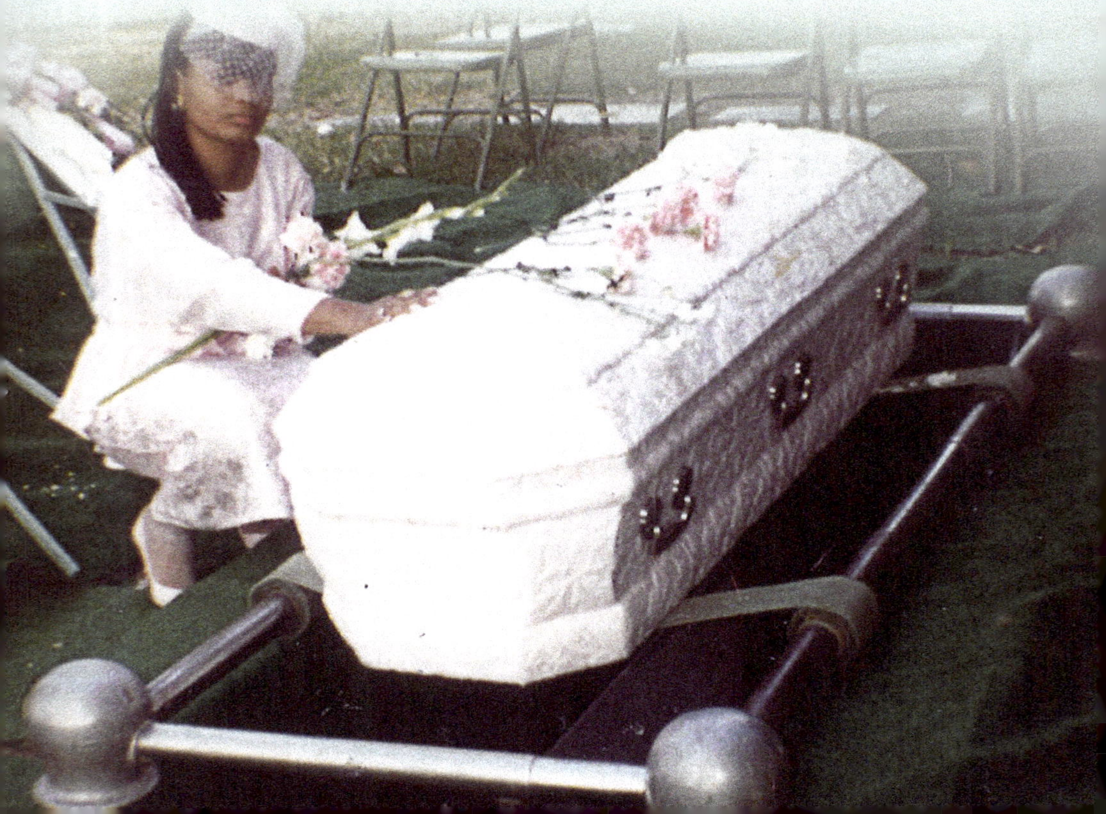

After the funeral, months later, I was in a very deep depression. I didn't want to comb my hair. I didn't want to go out of the house. I didn't want my youngest son Anthony (Truck) to start school. I was scared he was going to contract meningitis as well.

One day my next-door neighbor (an older lady), whom I had just met when I moved into my new neighborhood, came over to my house to give her condolences and check on me. She knocked on my door and said, "Hello, may I speak with Kathy?"

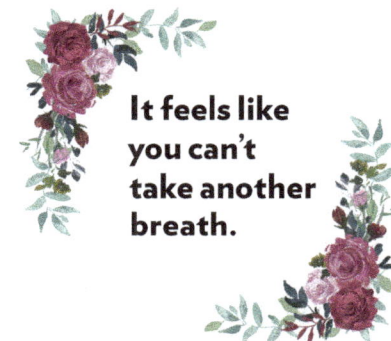

It feels like you can't take another breath.

I stepped out on the porch and said, "Yes, how can I help you?"

She said, "I'm your neighbor, and I heard about your daughter. I'm so sorry. I just want you to know that she's with the Lord, and she's OK."

Then she began to tell me about her pastor, Dr. Fred Price, and his wife Betty Price's experience with the loss of their child. She shared their testimony with me on how they coped with it through prayer and faith in God. For the first time since my daughter's death, I began to feel a little comfort. I thanked her as she left me a Bible. It was a breath of fresh air to my soul, but I was still angry with God.

The weeks turned into months. It was almost a year, and I still didn't want to clean out my daughter's closet or remove any of her things. I dared anyone to touch any of her belongings because I could still smell her through her clothes as I lay on her bed and cried myself to sleep. So much pain and trauma had consumed my heart, mind, body, soul, and spirit. I was like a walking dead woman. I was slowly trying to detach myself from my feelings just to survive.

What Ifs

I had so many questions in my head after my daughter's death, all the "what ifs." What if I had done this? Or what if I had done that? What if? What if? What if? The what ifs were driving me crazy! I had no peace. I recall getting my gun and locking myself in the bathroom thinking about ending my life. The inner torment and pain were too excruciating for me to live with. But I thought about my son, Anthony Jr. (Truck). His face kept flashing before me. What would happen to him if I did it?

I had a second chance to get it right.

My brother Ronnie knocked on the bathroom door, "Hey, Sis, you have been in there for a long time!" He heard me crying, bust through the bathroom door, and took the gun from me. He held me as I cried until I fell asleep in his arms.

Incidentally, when Ronnie was released from prison, he totally turned his life around by the help of the Lord. Starting all over again he picked up the pieces of a trade he once knew as a young man again and began working on cars and selling them. This trade afforded him the finances to purchase a beautiful home and now his own body shop. He also ministers to young boys and men sharing his life challenges and journey. I am so proud of the person he is today.

Speaking of new beginnings...

About a year after the bathroom incident, my ex-boyfriend was released from jail on a furlough pass for a few days. I recall him saying, "I'm getting a divorce." Lies—again. He pleaded with me not to leave him. "I will give you another beautiful daughter," he said. At this point in my life, I was weak and vulnerable. And yes, I had a beautiful baby girl. Although nothing or no one could ever replace my daughter Kuleshia, it was a joy to know I had a second chance to get it right. Shortly after birthing my beautiful baby girl, I named her Kierra Unique because she was unique, feisty, and strong. She became the air beneath my wings. Anthony and Kierra now gave me life and hope again.

My mother had been living with me temporarily after Kuleshia's death. Now she was asking if she could stay with me because she had nowhere to go. Without hesitation, I said, "Yes, you can stay with me." My son Anthony Jr., my little protector, and Kierra, my little princess, became my world. I had hope for my family again. But even now, years and years later, I still find myself missing and longing for Kuleshia. The loss of a loved one is never easy. Getting through such losses takes time. Kuleshia's birthdays remain the hardest days to deal with. But God has given me peace that surpasses all my understanding.

This little princess Kierra had everybody's attention. She was loved and spoiled, and she knew it! She turned one, then two years old, and was so smart I put her in the Head Start program at two and a half years old. Then I enrolled in Suzanne's Beauty College, graduated, and tried to make legal money. No more drug dealing or prostitution for me. I was done. I had always loved doing hair, as my grandmother and mother were both hairstylists.

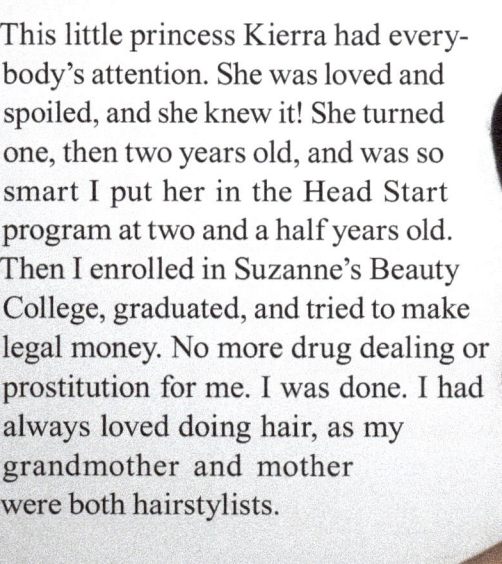

Me graduating from Suzanne Beauty College – 1988

CHAPTER 7

WRONG RIB

It was also time for me to make up my mind. What was I going to do about the adulterous relationship I was in? Nothing had changed for the better. And it wasn't OK with me anymore. My grandparents pleaded with me to get out of the relationship because God had something better for me. I was ready to make some changes, and people were praying for me to make them. I was finally regaining my strength. After all, it's never OK to date married men. I tell women all the time, don't do it! It's a no-win game. Just for a second, stop and put yourself in the wife's shoes.

Oftentimes, as women, we become so selfish and self-centered we only think about me, myself, and I. We never consider the feelings of another woman and her home being interrupted by our selfishness. But I thank God I woke up and began to see the relationship for what it really was—lust not love. My beautiful daughter Kierra was two years old, and I had finally come to my senses. It seemed as if after the death of my daughter Kuleshia, I slowly began to change. The morals, principles, and values I was taught by my grandparents were all coming back to my memory.

Thank You, Mrs. Lee

The lady who lived next door, Mrs. Lee, ministered to me frequently. She was a sweet, precious angel put in my life at the time I needed it

BROKEN BEYOND RECOGNITION

most. Mrs. Lee prayed with me and read the Bible to me but never overdid it. She did just enough to get me through and keep me coming back.

Values taught by my grandparents were all coming back.

I soon moved from that house and never saw her again. A couple of years later, I returned just to tell her thank you once again as I often told her, but she wasn't there any longer. She had moved. Mrs. Lee lived on 107th Street and Yukon in Inglewood in 1986. To her, I say thank you for watering the seed.

Finally, I ended the adulterous relationship for good then moved where he couldn't find me until the tie was broken. I never looked back. The lies, deception, and betrayal were all over. Keep your money and gifts. I'm done. I felt free from that relationship, and my life was changing for the better. I was cleaning the house! I didn't have words to describe what I was feeling. All I knew is that it felt good inside, and the things I once enjoyed, I had no desire to do anymore. I had no real interest in them. Someone was truly praying to God for me.

Me changing for the better and modeling – 1989

During this same time, cards and letters were still being sent to my grandparents' house for me. Even years later, people would stop by to encourage me. I will never forget the outpouring of love I received. Those from the hospital where my daughter passed away, her school friends, as well as the community all embraced me with so much love. I know their prayers helped to get me through. But now it was all about me and my two little ones, Anthony Jr. and Kierra. I kept them well taken care of and close to me.

The Pause Button

I put dating on pause because I still wasn't healed from the pain of my previous relationship. I had been with him for some years. I still wanted to beat up my old homeboy for introducing me to my ex. Lots of really nice single guys were serious and very much in love with me, but I had settled for last. Ladies, don't settle! He said all the right things and took very good care of me, but I chose to walk away from it all. I told him it was over. I meant every word of it. Look, I know today social media has normalized infidelity. But it's not OK!

I slowly began dating other guys, but my heart was broken and stone cold. I was salty toward men for a while. I started playing men like they were playing women. I had plenty and didn't care about any—sad to say. But sometimes falling out of love can hurt you so bad that it turns your heart cold. It desensitizes you. Now I tell young women, if he is married, look for the red flags and run for your life. I tell the married women to make their husbands accountable to them for the nights they don't come home. Perhaps if it was not so easy for my ex to stay out all night for weeks at a time, I may have picked up the signs sooner that he was married. However, at that time, that might not have made much of a difference because I was totally lost.

Ladies, you must know your worth. At that time in my life, I didn't know mine. You are valuable and deserve the best. You deserve to be someone's wife, not a side piece or chick. After getting out of that relationship, I went to his wife and asked her for genuine forgiveness. I felt I owed her an apology. I was changing; something was happening to me for the better, and I liked it! We talked like two mature women, and she said, "Kathy, I knew about you a long time ago, but I didn't fault you because you couldn't have done any more than he allowed you to! I accept your apology." That felt good as my morals were coming back. We hugged, and from that day on I never dated married men again. I had learned a valuable lesson to never compromise my morals, values, and integrity at the expense of hurting others.

I felt I owed her an apology.

After graduating from beauty college, I worked in a salon and in my home doing hair. If you sat in my chair, you were definitely walking out of it fly! Things had really started to look good for me and my two children. But I was still a long way from God. My mother was living with me and enjoying her grandchildren. It was as if she tried to make up for her wrongdoings through them. She was a much better grandmother than she was a mother. She would tell me, "Go out, Kathy, and have some fun."

But I would laugh and tell her, "I don't know! Because I know your kind of fun, lady."

She would just laugh and say, "I'm sorry, daughter, for leaving you and your siblings."

We had some very intimate conversations about her life and losing her mother at such a young age. We talked about her relationship with my father. She expressed that they really did love each other and their children but had lost their way to drinking alcohol and doing drugs. Many things she didn't know, my father taught her.

My mother opened up and poured out her heart to me. She asked for forgiveness for all the pain she and my father had caused my siblings and me. I could see she was still not healed from her abuse. Neither was I.

CHAPTER 8

HE FOUND HIS GOOD THING WOUNDED

Have you ever had those girlfriends who once you hooked up with them, you knew everything was going to be alright? Deloris, Debra, Myrna, Cookie, and Tammy all had my back, and I had theirs. My girl Delores (Duck) was my ride-or-die. If you saw me, you saw her! We went everywhere together. My grandfather named us 88 and 99.

My girlfriends Cookie, Myrna, Debra, and Tammy wouldn't let me be sad. They would say, "Let's go out." We would party all night until the next day. We had so much fun playing the guys as they were trying to play us. We drove luxury cars: Mercedes-Benz, Corvettes, and I drove a Jaguar. We were always fly: hair, nails, and clothes were on point.

I started dating another high roller who was showering me with expensive gifts. One day he invited me and my friends to join him and his friends, who were throwing him a big birthday party at a very well-known club. He asked if I would be his date. I said, "Only if I can bring my homegirls." He said, "Yes, sure." So I went and had a great time, but after a while I was over it and ready to go home.

Clubbing with my friends Robyn, Myrna, and Deloris – 1985

I told my girlfriend Cookie, whom I had driven there with that night, to take me home. She asked me if everything was alright. I said yes, I just want to go home. Truth is I didn't want this guy who invited me to think he had anything coming that night. In my mind, it wasn't the time for that. In any case, his account with me wasn't high enough! See, I had learned early how to keep the treasure chest closed until the timing was right.

Be a Challenge

Here's another nugget for women: stop sleeping with these men on the first date if you want a meaningful relationship. They will not value or respect you as a woman. Every man who wants to be married already has in the back of his mind what kind of woman he wants as a wife. And she is not the one who gave it up on the first date, trust me. Although most men will sleep with that kind, they are not taken seriously!

I recall my oldest brother schooling me back in the day. He had lots of women, so I asked him which one he really liked. He called a name, and I asked why her? He said she was a challenge and not easy to get like the others who chased him down. Wow! Think about that, ladies. Many women think they can freak their way sexually into a man's heart. No, it doesn't work like that. You were just a freak for a night! And although he may have enjoyed it, you still do not have wife status. So don't be mad when he drops you off with a Happy Meal and continues driving to seek a wife.

Don't be mad when he drops you off with a Happy Meal.

As Cookie and I started to leave the club that night, my date asked me if everything was OK and why I was leaving. He asked me not to go. I assured him everything was nice and said I would call him. But again, something was changing in me.

I Love Me Some Chocolate

As we traveled along, Cookie made a left turn onto Century Boulevard headed to my house. Out of nowhere, a beautiful black Mercedes-Benz S500 pulled up on my side of Cookie's car. I looked over my shoulder from the passenger's seat and saw a handsome man smiling at me. Cookie said, "Kat, do you know him?"

I said, "No, but he sure is cute with his chocolate self. Girl, you know I like them chocolate."

We laughed, but he was very persistent in trying to find out who I was. He signaled with his hands and lips for me to roll down my window. I did as he said, "What's your name?"

I answered, "Kathy."

He said, "Kathy, can you pull over so I can get your number?"

I was cautious because it was late, about 1:00 AM. We wanted to find a place where there was plenty of light, so we pulled over to a McDonald's, which was closed but the lighting was good on Century. The man drove up behind us. He got out of his car with this long superfly perm in his hair. That was pretty fly back then. I rolled down the window and gave him my number.

He said, "My name is LaFrance. Kathy, I live in the valley, but I'm down here visiting my mother."

I said, "OK, Lafrance. I have a female cousin named LaFrance as well, very unique name. Have a good night."

He said, "I sure hope this is the right number, Kathy."

I just smiled as we pulled off. I really didn't think much of him. He was cute, but I was past cute. So I added him to the list, but that black Benz was pretty fly. I was so lost. When I got home, the kids were asleep and my mom was watching TV.

"Kathy," she said. "Is that you?"

"Yes," I answered.

"Girl, this phone has been ringing off the hook and some new-name guy keeps calling. He said his name is LaFrance."

I smiled to myself. He was moving fast. He called again, and I answered.

"Oh, you didn't give me the wrong number after all."

I laughed, thinking to myself this dude is serious. I said, "No, I didn't."

He responded, "I made it to my mother's house. Can I come over to your house?"

"Oh, no!" I shouted out. "I just met you, and I have children who don't know you!"

He said, "I'll bring my mother with me."

"No! No!" I said. I was determined to do things differently than I had in the past.

"OK, I can respect that," he said.

Looking for More

Our conversation began on the phone and didn't end until about 5:00 AM. We talked and laughed like we had known each other for years. Normally, I would have been off the phone quickly, but something was different about this LaFrance guy. He was very open and candid about himself. He knew what he wanted in life and where he was headed. I liked that because he was one of the few who could actually tell me his plans. He seemed to be looking for more than a girlfriend. It sounded as if he was ready to settle down with someone and start a family. So I started backing up a little because I knew I had a lot of work to do on me. I couldn't take the mask off and reveal who I really was. I didn't know if I could be serious with anyone, and the process was just beginning.

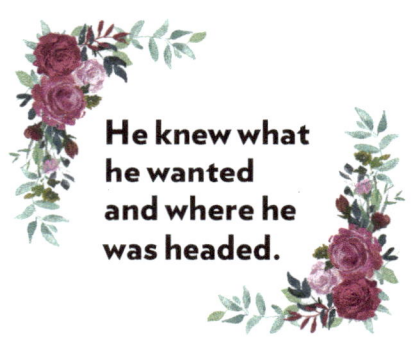

He knew what he wanted and where he was headed.

Lafrance continued to call, and after a few weeks I decided to take him up on a date. He picked me up, and we went to Tony's on the pier in Redondo Beach. We ordered so much seafood—way too much for just the two of us. He said from the moment he saw me I was what he wanted. He told me he had been married before, but it was a jailhouse marriage that wasn't built on true love but convenience. He also said he was divorced and was taking his time before remarrying again. I shared how I was coming out of a long relationship and was taking my time as well. He asked me if I would mind him calling his brother to come to the restaurant to help us eat up all the seafood. I said no, I didn't mind.

Shortly after, this tall young man walked in and introduced himself as Samuel, LaFrance's brother.

"Nice to meet you, Samuel. I'm Kathy."

He smiled and said he had heard a lot of positive things about me and that his brother wouldn't stop talking about me. I smiled.

LaFrance said, "Man, help us eat all this food. I think we overordered."

Samuel dove into the food, and we had an awesome time!

LaFrance became more persistent. He wanted to see me again, but I was a wounded woman hiding her bleeding really well—so I thought. I didn't want to jump into another relationship. But after about three months, the calls and dates became more frequent. Finally, I introduced him to my children and mother. Immediately, they took to him with his playful, friendly personality. He arranged activities for us to do as a family, but I became a bit hesitant. Wait. Hold up! I wasn't just seeing him. I was actually seeing other guys, some of whom were very serious about me. However, there was something special about LaFrance.

My mother began to get sicker. She suffered from diabetes and seizures, which she developed from the head blows she endured from my father. All her complications required a lot of medical attention, and I was trying to get her well while working in a salon doing hair. Tending to her was overbearing at times. So I asked my siblings for help, and together we did our best for the woman who left us behind. During this stressful time, LaFrance was getting more serious. He was proving himself to be a man of his word. He was honest about his son, LaFrance Jr., from a previous relationship whom he had gotten full custody of.

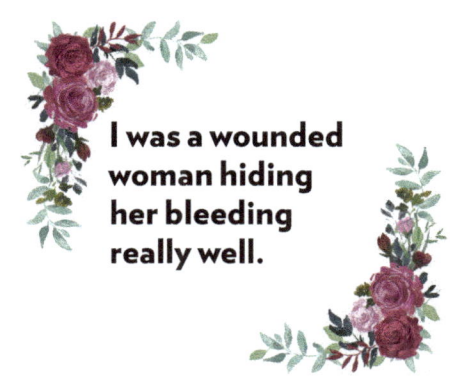

I was a wounded woman hiding her bleeding really well.

He asked me if I would meet his mother. I did. I remember the first time I met her. Betty is her name. She looked me up and down as if she didn't know what my purpose or motive was with her son.

BROKEN BEYOND RECOGNITION

I'm not sure if she liked me or not. I was draped in lots of gold chains, gold rings, had long nails, flawless hair—the whole fly girl thing! So I could respect that; however, as time went by, we became the best of friends, as well as mother and daughter-in-law. She has been a big inspiration for me. She always has a listening ear to hear and gives me the very best advice. I love her dearly.

His mother assured me he was not married and hadn't been for over a year. But I still wanted to see her son's divorce papers first before I made any decision. I was not going to repeat my past mistakes.

LaFrance told me he wanted us to be more than friends. He said he did not want to share me with anyone. I was honest that I was seeing other guys, and I really just wanted to be friends. But after a while, LaFrance had outdone them all. His patience with me was amazing. I dropped all the others one by one until the list was clean. Still, he did not know a lot about me. He had no idea about my inner turmoil and past.

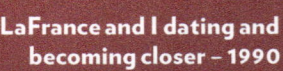

LaFrance and I dating and becoming closer – 1990

But First the Story

After about six months, LaFrance proposed a couple of times. Eventually I said yes! But I first had to share my past with him. I told him I had been through a lot and done a lot of things that I wasn't proud of. But now I was trying to heal from some things. After hours of sharing everything, he just looked at me and said, "I still want to marry you because there is a diamond under all that dirt. I'm going to find it." He asked me if I wanted a big wedding. I said no, so we went to a little chapel in downtown Los Angeles and got married in 1991.

LaFrance was just what I needed: a strong man who had no problem putting me in my place. He was honest, truthful, and loved me with my many flaws. He had come from a lifestyle similar to mine and had overcome a lot of difficulties himself. But God was doing something so unique in us. It was as if I had a very best friend who was there to help me better my life. He also helped me with my mother's doctor appointments and took the kids back and forth to school while we both worked all at the same time. This was too good to be true, but it was true. God had sent me a good man.

My mother thought the world of LaFrance. She was so happy about my new love. Unfortunately, shortly after we married, she died of heart failure. I was in deep pain again. I was broken, but this time I had a strong shoulder to cry on. LaFrance was there every step of the way. I had peace in knowing I had done my very best for my mother before she died. I had also led her to the Lord with the sinner's prayer that I remembered from my auntie and uncle's church.

> **LaFrance was just what I needed.**

If the death of my mother wasn't enough, my grandparents who raised me died one right after the other. My husband was right there with me through it all. It seemed as if God knew those three people were going to depart, and I would not survive if my husband wasn't there to carry me through three deaths in a matter of two years.

LaFrance supporting me as one of my mother's pallbearers – 1994

CHAPTER 9

THE INVITES JUST WOULDN'T STOP

LaFrance and I had talked about church and how we were raised there, but both of us had strayed so far away from it. Soon after my mother's death, my cousin Loretta invited us to visit her church for a special service they were having. At first I said no. I hadn't been to church in years, but she kept inviting us over and over. She was so relentless we decided to go just to stop her from asking. I'm glad we did.

I was preparing for my mother's funeral, and at the same time I was getting ready to visit Loretta's church, Trinity Chapel on Wilmington Avenue in Compton. I thought I was doing her a favor by accepting the invitation. Little did I know God was setting my husband and me up to get to know Him as Lord and Savior. We gathered our children, Anthony, LaFrance Jr., and Kierra, and headed to Loretta's church. At that time, I was pregnant with my daughter Kamerra.

It was such a beautiful atmosphere where the people were kind and friendly. The pastor and his wife made us feel right at home. The message from the pastor spoke directly to our hearts. I wanted to ask my cousin if she told her pastor any of my business because it seemed as though he was speaking directly to me. Now I understand the work of the Holy Spirit when He is moving. He uses the vessel to minister to the people and their situations. He knows exactly where we are in our lives.

Finally, it was over, and I was glad because sinners can only take a little bit of church at a time. Laughing out loud! I figured now maybe my cousin Loretta wouldn't ask us to visit her church anymore. However, about a week or two later, Pastor Edward T. Robinson Sr. of Trinity Chapel reached out to my husband and me. He invited us to return and fellowship with them. We said we would visit again soon.

It was time to deliver our beautiful baby girl, Kamerra, whom we nicknamed MeMe. She brought us even closer in our marriage. We were overjoyed. She had big bright eyes, and we were surprised at how long she was: 23 inches. My husband said she was going to be tall. Today she *is* tall—5'10" and a professional model.

Shortly after her birth, my husband and I took the pastor up on his invitation and visited the church quite frequently. They sang songs I hadn't heard in years that I used to sing as a young girl coming up in my Aunt Eloise and Uncle George's church. This Trinity Chapel church began to really make us feel at home. They loved our children and embraced us all as a family. It felt so good. The Lord began to move mightily in my life. It was as if I had come full circle to where I was predestined to be.

I had come full circle to where I was predestined to be.

Me, LaFrance, and our new family
Anthony Jr., LaFrance Jr., and Kierra – 1993

What Was Right

We joined the church in 1994, and from that point on my life changed drastically. I was finished with the partying scene but still had a long way to go. Most of my friends and family wondered what was wrong with me. Many said I was crazy and had lost my mind. But it wasn't what was wrong with me; it was what was right with me! I was connecting to the greater me within.

I recall one Sunday at church the Word of God really ministered to my heart as it was being preached so profoundly. Tears flowed from my eyes. I fought hard to hold them back as Pastor Robinson said, "If you are tired and need to be free, come." I got out of my seat and headed to the altar with a spirit of repentance and brokenness. I was tired. The pain and suffering were too much for me to carry. I told God how sorry I was for my sins that were many. Like the woman with the alabaster box, I went to Jesus just as I was—broken. I repented for blaming Him for my daughter's death and my childhood trauma.

All of a sudden, a deep, overwhelming sense of love surrounded my entire being inside and out like a blanket of love. I stood there crying for what seemed like hours and hours while the mothers of the church ministered to me. I was caught up in this beautiful cleansing place with the Lord. It felt as if someone had a huge brush gently scrubbing away all my dark hurts, pains, abandonment, disappointment, frustration, bitterness, anger, pride, and rejection. Wow! I was finally getting the help I desperately needed. It all seemed right as I walked back to my seat with my mascara running down my face, hair all over the place, and nose dripping. I was getting set free. I felt I belonged with the saints of God. I wasn't sure if my husband had experienced the same thing I did, but to my surprise, he was in tears as well. God was moving upon him too.

After leaving the church, we felt very good and refreshed as we shared the message preached that day and how it pertained to our lives. However, we were not as free as we thought. We were still very carnal-minded. We would go to the same old liquor store and get some of the same old alcohol and cigarettes, put some meat on the grill, and continue in our sinful lifestyles.

Nevertheless, the process of deliverance had begun. We did this until one Sunday in 1995 on New Year's Eve. We were at church that night, which was very unusual for us! New Year's Eve, we were definitely going to be at somebody's nightclub or party bringing in the New Year, but not this particular year.

Pastor Robinson had called in a powerful evangelist to speak at the New Year's Eve service. For the first time, we were going to spend New Year's Eve in the house of the Lord. The service began as our church choir "Oracles" led us in worship and praise. It was much better than any nightclub, and I didn't have a hangover the next day. Everyone was extremely happy. The atmosphere was rich with the presence of the Lord. I lifted my hands in worship unto God.

The Gift

The evangelist got up to speak from the book of Acts on the power of the Holy Ghost. He had my full attention. By the time he got to the end of his sermon, he asked who wanted to be baptized and filled with the Holy Ghost and power. I jumped up and ran to the altar with everyone else. My husband was right beside me. Our hands were lifted high as God baptized me in the Holy Ghost with the evidence of speaking in tongues. The power of God was so strong yet so beautiful. I knew I had received the gift! Sometime later, we all returned to our seats.

As the service came to a close, my husband said, "I asked God, but I didn't get it." The evangelist had said some of us might receive it on our way home, when we got home, or even later. It all depended on when God was ready to give it to us. So my husband decided to continue praising the Lord until he got it. We arrived home, and as we were getting ready for bed, LaFrance was still praising the Lord. Then he began mumbling something. He got louder and louder, and all of a sudden the tongues began to flow out of his belly like a river of living water. It was uncontrollable and lasted for hours. He cried and praised the Lord until I jumped back into the river with him. We spoke in tongues and worshiped the Lord all night long!

He was doing a new thing in our lives.

The following Sunday when we returned to church, we were very excited about this new indwelling power of the Holy Ghost. God was delivering us. However, after service, we tried to do our little usual—go to the liquor store and get a drink of alcohol. But the Holy Ghost wasn't having it! We got so sick after drinking and felt really bad as the Lord revealed to us He was doing a new thing in our lives.

The power of the Holy Spirit is real. We began to hunger and thirst for God day and night, night and day, from Sunday morning service to Wednesday night Bible studies. We were there soaking up the Word of God. I recall asking the Lord to deliver me from every man I had ever slept with. I no longer wanted the soul ties, dreams, and visions of my past that were haunting me. See, the devil always brought back memories of the old sexual relationships I had while I was trying to do the right thing in my new marriage. The Bible speaks of soul ties. It says he who unites with a harlot becomes one with her (1 Corinthians 6:16). Then I asked the Lord to help me forgive my parents for all the pain and trauma they caused my siblings and me.

Surgical Instructions

The Spirit of the Lord gave me detailed instructions for deliverance. He instructed me to go into my dining room alone, get down on my knees, and pray to my heavenly Father. The next step was to denounce every act of sexual intercourse I ever had with a man outside of my marriage. After that, I had to forgive my parents for the hurt and pain they caused me. That one was hard because the pain was deep down in the crevices of my soul, but I wanted to be free. I was fully aware of what was going on. The Holy Spirit was working on me like a surgeon. Lastly, He told me to forgive myself and release my daughter's death into His hands. I broke down to nothing as I followed this instruction.

The Holy Spirit gently tilted my head back as the demonic spirits began to leave me like Pac-Man. My mouth opened. I screamed and collapsed on the floor. My husband said when he walked into the room, he knew God was working on me. I was under the power of the Holy Spirit as the "Great Physician" was doing surgery. My husband said only my belly was moving as tears were running out from my eyes. The Lord instructed him not to touch me because I was being delivered.

After a couple of hours, I got up feeling light, empty, and hollow inside. Days later, the feelings of unforgiveness, anger, bitterness, and the dreams of other sexual relationships were all gone. He immediately told me to read the New and Old Testaments. The Holy Spirit became my teacher, teaching me words I once couldn't pronounce.

New Region For Christ

About two years after sitting under the Holy Spirit's teaching, my husband and I heard God calling us to open a Bible study in our home in 1996. He gave us the name of the study in a dream: "New Region For Christ" (Acts 13:49). The Lord told us it would be a ministry where people would get delivered and set free. We asked our Pastor Robinson if it was OK, and he said yes. However, he assigned spiritual leaders to oversee us. We were so excited our hearts were burning with passion, joy, faith, and expectation. We were eager to share the gospel and tell people there is a God Who loves them unconditionally. In spite of what we have done, He loves us.

Pastor Robinson called LaFrance and me into his office one Sunday after service. He explained he had assigned Elder Cardell Candler, one of the elders in the church, to oversee us in our Bible study. Looking back, it was a wise decision our pastor made to keep us accountable and to make sure we were teaching sound doctrine. He knew we were very zealous about God but needed to grow more and become seasoned in the Word. What I really loved about our pastor was he never killed our vision or passion to see souls saved.

Shortly after we began the Bible studies, our family and friends accepted the invitation to come. As we shared the good news, the gospel of Jesus Christ, people were saved and filled with the Holy Spirit with the evidence of speaking in tongues right in our home. Even my mother-in-law, Betty, was baptized in the Holy Spirit. Elder Candler was at every Bible study. Once a week, he would come over to our house and personally teach my husband and me more of the Word of God. He would bring maps, charts, and diagrams, which he laid out and explained to us in a way we could understand. This man is anointed with such wisdom, understanding, knowledge, revelation, and power.

Some days, Elder Candler would sit on our front porch and minister to my husband and me for hours at a time. He would answer all the questions we had. It was as if he was spoon-feeding us as you do a baby. We would eat it all up! He would always say God was preparing my husband and me for great things, and He was going to use us mightily. We received it, but the enemy was still bringing condemnation from my past to stop me from fulfilling

God's purpose for my life. He bombarded my mind with thoughts that God could never use me because of my past. But being so in love with God, I didn't let that stop me.

A Bat Out of Hell

The enemy tried again to stop me in ministry by bringing fear through a demonic dream. It was after an anointed foot-washing service that my husband and I attended one night. When we got home, I fell into a deep sleep the likes of which I had never experienced. In the dream, I recall falling deeper into this dark tunnel where I could see nothing but small little lights that were green, red, and yellow—almost like Christmas lights. Other than those little lights, I could see nothing. Terror was all around me and a voice kept telling me to come deeper down into the dark tunnel, but I wouldn't because I was now full of fear and wouldn't move. Then the voice began to chant "Chesus! Chesus!" I thought it was saying "Jesus! Jesus!" So I began to follow it deeper down into the dark tunnel.

I could see my body on the floor as I began to hover over it. The demonic voice now seemed to have control over me. Suddenly, a loud voice that I recognized spoke full of power and authority, saying, "Katherine, come out!" But I couldn't move my body. The voice I recognized spoke again and said, "Call on the name of JESUS and plead the BLOOD! Come out, Katherine!" I kept following the voice of the Lord, calling on the name of JESUS and pleading the blood of Jesus.

My husband said he jumped up out of the bed and grabbed the anointing oil and began praying over me. He said I seemed to be in a struggle and wouldn't wake up. The voice of the Lord stayed with me until I opened my eyes. Once I opened my eyes, I saw my husband praying over me and saying, "Kathy, wake up! Wake up!"

When I woke, I saw a huge, black, demonic bat about 8 feet tall jump off of me and run through my back bedroom door. I immediately jumped up out of the bed and began vomiting. As I ran to the bathroom, I noticed that my feet and hands were white as if there had been no blood circulation. I stood there trying to tell my husband what had just happened to me, that a demonic presence had just visited me. But all I could do was cry and worship the Lord for leading me out of that dark place.

Days and weeks later, I still was thanking and praising God for bringing me out. I asked the Lord, "Why did You allow me to go through that?" He said, "Because I want you to know that the enemy is a real force and without Me you are no competition. But through Me, you can do all things. I have not given you a spirit of fear, but of power, and of love, and of a sound mind" (2 Timothy 1:7). Then the Lord said to me, "Daughter, I have given you authority to trample on snakes and scorpions and to overcome all the power of the enemy; nothing will harm you" (Luke 10:19).

Saints of Value

A friend of mine named Debra introduced me to a powerful woman of God by the name of Dr. Vickie Lee who had a training center called Saints of Value (S.O.V.). My husband and I joined her hands-on training center. This powerful woman of God, who has since gone on to be with the Lord, helped us learn how to win souls to the Lord correctly. She would take us to the Union Rescue Mission in downtown Los Angeles to minister to the homeless, pray for them, and feed them food. We learned hands-on ministry and so much more from this anointed vessel of God.

After graduating from S.O.V. Training Center, God seemed to be moving very fast with us. Still, we remained accountable to our Pastor Robinson and our mentor, Elder Candler at all times. We faithfully attended church at Trinity Chapel, our home church, every Sunday. My husband LaFrance heard from the Lord for us to have a two-day down-home revival right in the backyard of our home. We rented chairs, tents, and had anointed speakers join us.

We also wanted to feed the people, so we asked God to provide us with the money and food to do so, and He did. He multiplied the food so much that we had to give a lot of it away. It was much more than we needed! The revival was a success and powerful! Lots of people were in our backyard crying out to God to be saved. It was an amazing sight to see.

In 1998, I became pregnant. I recall the Lord telling me my baby would be a boy and I should name him Joshua because he would lead the family. My doctor confirmed I was carrying a boy, and, yes, I named him Joshua. He has brought so much joy into our lives. After Joshua was about two years old, LaFrance and I decided to go back to school. This time we enrolled in Esther Mallet Bible University where we really got deep into biblical theology. We graduated in 2002 with AA degrees in biblical theology.

Our plates were full of parenting, working jobs, and doing ministry. Pastor Robinson sat us down and said it was evident God's hand was upon our lives for ministry. He felt God was going to use us to even be pastors one day, but he told us to wait on God. This was no surprise because the Lord had been waking my husband and me out of our sleep and speaking expressly to us that we were called to be pastors.

After many years of evangelizing and training God's people, it seemed as if New Region For Christ was over as the Bible studies were no more. We became very involved in assisting our pastor until 2012, when we were awakened by the Lord telling us, "Now is the time." He was saying it was time to start the local church. And do you know what He called it? Yes! New Region For Christ. The rest is history as NRFC is a powerful church today in 2020. The Holy Ghost is alive and well!

> *Very truly I tell you, unless a kernel of wheat falls to the ground and dies, it remains only a single seed. But if it dies, it produces many seeds. (John 12:24, NIV)*

CHAPTER 10

DON'T LOSE YOUR MIND; YOU'RE GONNA NEED IT

Looking back now, I can testify that I should have lost my mind, but destiny wouldn't let me. In retrospect, I was responding to life with a victim mentality. I had to first get my mind delivered from my past, which was tormenting and stopping me from moving into my future. The Bible tells us to be renewed in our minds. I did this by giving my life to God first. Then I finally understood through the Word of God that my mind was the battleground where the enemy was fighting and defeating me. But through the Word of God, I learned how to take a stand in my new position as a believer. Every believer is a *new creature* in Christ. It was time to transform my mind.

> *And be not conformed to this world: but be ye transformed by the renewing of your mind, that ye may prove what is that good, and acceptable, and perfect, will of God.*
> *(Romans 12:2)*

> *Therefore, with minds that are alert and fully sober, set your hope on the grace to be brought to you when Jesus Christ is revealed at his coming. (1 Peter 1:13)*

I decided to start winning the battles in my mind. The Bible says as a man thinks, so is he (Proverbs 23:7). Therefore, I had to get rid of all the negative, stinking thinking I had been trained by the insecurities, pain, fears, and doubts of my past to believe. I had to tell myself I am who God says I am! What we think, say, and believe about ourselves drives us. The way we talk to ourselves can empower or disempower us. Negative self-talk can weaken us and make us feel we have no control over our lives. But speaking the Word of God over our lives empowers us. I started analyzing all the thoughts that entered my mind and took authority over them. Everything that didn't pass the test had to go!

> *Therefore if any man be in Christ, he is a new creature: old things are passed away; behold, all things are become new.*
> *(2 Corinthians 5:17)*

> *Casting down imaginations, and every high thing that exalteth itself against the knowledge of God, and bringing into captivity every thought to the obedience of Christ.*
> *(2 Corinthians 10:5)*

I would embrace the thought or cast it down!

I had work to do. I asked myself these three questions:

- Was this thought sent to *better* me or *condemn* me?
- Was this thought the truth according to my *new identity* in Christ Jesus?
- Who was the *sender* of this thought?

Once I recognized and identified the source by answering these three questions, I would make my decision to embrace the thought or cast it down!

Victorious Survivor

Whatever you have been through, do not continue to think of yourself as a victim. Instead, think of yourself as a victorious survivor. The next time you feel fearful, angry, and powerless, tell yourself, "I'm very much in control, and I can do all things through Christ who gives me the ability!"

> *No, in all these things we are more than conquerors through him who loved us. (Roman 8:37, NIV)*

> *Death and life are in the power of the tongue: and they that love it shall eat the fruit thereof. (Proverbs 18:21)*

> *A good man brings good things out of the good stored up in his heart, and an evil man brings evil things out of the evil stored up in his heart. For the mouth speaks what the heart is full of. (Luke 6:45, NIV)*

We all think of ourselves as being pretty good people. But we must realize our nature is inherently evil and wicked. We harbor evil thoughts in our hearts. It is only by the grace of God and the covering of Jesus Christ that we are seen as good through His eyes.

Jesus reminds us that our speech and actions will reveal what is in our hearts. And whether our thoughts are good or bad, they roll off our tongues with ease. Oftentimes when people say, "I'm sorry; I didn't mean to say that!" I say, "Yes, you did, because that's what's in your heart, and your mouth spoke it!"

Do you remember what your mom used to tell you? "If you can't say something nice about someone, then don't say anything at all." This was good, godly advice.

> *Finally, brothers and sisters, whatever is true, whatever is noble, whatever is right, whatever is pure, whatever is lovely, whatever is admirable—if anything is excellent or praiseworthy—think about such things. (Philippians 4:8, NIV)*

There is a well-known slogan that says, "A Mind Is a Terrible Thing to Waste"—how true this is. But it's also a wonderful thing to invest in. I found out that there is real peace for one's mind when it is anchored in the Word of God.

> *You will keep in perfect peace those whose minds are steadfast, because they trust in you. (Isaiah 26:3, NIV)*

> *Set your minds on things above, not on earthly things. (Colossians 3:2, NIV)*

> *Let this mind be in you, which was also in Christ Jesus. (Philippians 2:5)*

The same old thoughts you have held in your mind tend to occur in your life. If you continue to think you are defeated, you will always act as if you are defeated! Remember this:

> *For as he thinketh in his heart, so is he. (Proverbs 23:7a)*

Destroy those stronghold thoughts! Because whatever gets your mind gets you as well. So it is important that you guard, strengthen, and renew your mind. That's where the battle always starts.

> *Do not be anxious about anything, but in every situation, by prayer and petition, with thanksgiving, present your requests to God. And the peace of God, which transcends all understanding, will guard your hearts and your minds in Christ Jesus. (Philippians 4:6-7)*

CHAPTER 11

DESTINY'S DAUGHTER

At the beginning of my ministry, stepping out in faith into my destiny was challenging. The first thing that hit me was fear! It tried to paralyze me into believing the old lies of fear and doubt. The devil never wants us to know who we are in God. But by this time, I was walking in the power of the Holy Spirit. My spiritual eyes were now opened, and I approached my destiny in my new position in Christ Jesus. I stood up in an offensive position, not the old defeated position, because I was a new creature in Christ Jesus. That's how I approached everything in my life.

I've come to realize that everything I experienced over the years prepared me for my ministry. I didn't have to fear at all because God has not given me a spirit of fear but of power, love, and a sound mind. Stepping into my destiny was not by might or power but by His Spirit! So everything I did in ministry was not by my ability but by instruction and the leading and power of the Holy Spirit, which made it so much easier for me.

One of the first things I tell young believers is don't try to be something you're not! Don't try to operate in an office God has not chosen you for because it can become a huge struggle and is also very dangerous. However, when God has called you to a specific office, it will be evident. Good pastors, spiritual fathers, spiritual mothers, and mentors can be great assets in this area. Most mature leaders can help direct new ministers in how to appropriately use their gifts.

Me in worship to the God Who set me free! – 1995

My very first speaking engagement for S.O.V. supported by LaFrance and Pastor Robinson – 1997

It was obvious God had chosen me for something much greater than I could imagine, and the work was ready to begin. I stepped out in faith and followed the leading of the Holy Spirit. I was invited to be a guest speaker for Saints of Value World Ministries by Dr. Vickie Lee. From that point forward, I was invited to many churches. I was in such demand that Pastor Robinson explained he didn't want my gift to take me places too fast that my character couldn't keep me in. He taught me the importance of integrity and how to walk in it. He told me to regard the church with five members just as important as the one with five hundred. He gave me a mop bucket, rag, and some cleaning soaps to clean the bathrooms and kitchen in the church. He warned me to beware of pride creeping in. He said the anointing on my life would bring me before great men and women, but I must always remain humble. He reminded me I was just a vessel being used, which is an honor, but all the glory belongs to God!

Me in the black robe of an ordained evangelist – 1997

Bouquets for Jesus

He reminded me to remain humble because God resists the proud but gives grace to the humble. He also said many will be delivered and set free, and in gratitude they will lift me up with words of roses. However, after I have spoken and the people flood around me, I should collect all the roses one by one and make beautiful bouquets out of them for Jesus, to Whom they belong.

I was walking in the office of an evangelist but still felt God was calling me to work with the young girls at our church. I expressed this to my pastor, who placed me over the True Love Waits program there at the church designed to help young girls remain abstinent before marriage.

All callings depend on God's grace, not our abilities. God knows you better than you know yourself. He called you to do what He knows He can enable you to do as you depend on His grace, not on your ability. Every time I depend on my ability, I get into trouble.

> *Trust in the Lord with all your heart and lean not on your own understanding; in all your ways submit to him, and he will make your paths straight. (Proverbs 3:5-6, NIV)*

The glorious fact about God's calling on our lives is that God gave it to us in Christ before time began. That's right! It was ours before there was a world where God created anything! He knew you and me. He had a plan for us before the world started. Look at how important we are to Him. God has a special plan and purpose for every one of us. And it started in eternity. If you go to Romans chapter 8, you will find three things that took place in eternity as it relates to you and me.

1. God foreknew us.
2. He chose us.
3. He predestined us.

All callings depend on God's grace, not our abilities.

No, you were not an accident waiting to happen or here by coincidence. God knew you before you knew you. He chose and predestined you before the foundation of the world.

After sharing this information with you, would you like to take a bold step and affirm God's calling for your life? If so, let's do it together right now with the following proclamation and prayer:

Heavenly Father, I come to You in the name of Your dear Son Jesus Christ, Who died on the cross for me. Forgive me of all my sins. I also ask You, Jesus Christ, to come into my heart and be my Lord and Savior. Lord, You have pulled me out of the fire all around me. You have a redemptive purpose and plan for my life. I also understand the adversary is working overtime trying to prevent me from coming into the fullness of Your plan for my life. I confess, Lord, that at various times through my own disobedience and sin I have fallen short and messed up the process of fulfilling Your purpose for my life. I come to You now in total honesty and transparency. Forgive me for allowing my own sin and the accusations from the enemy to deter me from my destiny in You. I know You are watching over me even now. Your eyes are upon me, not in condemnation but with every intention to cleanse me and renew Your awesome calling for me. By faith, I have received Jesus Christ into my heart as my Lord and Savior. By faith, I renounce the lies of the enemy, which have held me back. I am not an accident waiting to happen. I am a new creature in Christ Jesus! And by faith, I now take a bold step into God's plans and purposes for my life. I will mark this day as the beginning of a new season in my life and a fresh start to fulfill God's destiny for me. In Jesus' name. Amen!

God knew you before you knew you.

CHAPTER 12

TAKE THE WOMEN TO THE WELL

My husband and I were overseeing lots of ministries in and outside the church. I was an evangelist with many speaking engagements and the overseer of the young girls' group True Love Waits at our home church. My husband was an armorbearer for our Pastor Robinson for over fifteen years. We were also overseers for the church's married couples' ministry while working full time and raising five children. But after a few years, I began to feel a pull in my spirit that God was calling me to another assignment. It wouldn't stop. I began to have dreams and visions of me ministering to hurting, broken women. I couldn't shake it! I recall being in the shower and the voice of the Lord said, "I've called you to minister to the hurting women." I washed the soap off my face and said, "Lord, do You see how busy I am? I barely have the time for anything."

I tried to ignore that voice. I blocked it out and even made a deal with God to just let me evangelize churches. However, He meant what He said. It was a stretch for me. One particular Sunday at our home church, Trinity Chapel, our pastor invited a guest speaker from Hawaii by the name of Prophet John Harke. I never thought there would be anything unusual about church that Sunday or the invitation because we often had visiting speakers at our church. But, to my surprise, something was very different about that day and this speaker whom I had never met or seen in my life!

That same morning before going to church, my husband and I were undecided and had a conversation about what to wear. It was as if there were an interruption. We were stuck in a hard decision about what to wear. That's something we have never done! Anyway, we decided to dress alike in our red blazers, which we often did. However, before leaving the house, I told my husband I didn't like the way the red blazer looked on me. I said, "I think we should wear our yellow blazers instead." So we quickly changed into our yellow blazers and rushed out of the house.

Deliver This Word

We got to church, and sure enough this young man by the name of Prophet John Harke was there to minister the Word of God. Our pastor got up to introduce the speaker and his beautiful wife, Meleana. As they went up to the pulpit, the speaker's wife did an anointed Hawaiian dance of worship and then he spoke. Immediately, I discerned the anointing of God upon him. I could see the light of God shining brightly through him. About twenty minutes into his message, he stopped and said, "The Lord wants me to release this message now to a woman here with a yellow jacket on. Before I left home to come, the Lord told me to deliver this word to her and that she would be here."

The church was filled with people, and everyone started looking around, including me. We were all trying to figure out who this woman was. Then he pointed to me and asked me to stand. It was so obvious; I was the only woman there with a yellow jacket on, so I stood up as the prophetic message to me was released. It rolled from the prophet like a river. I don't recall it word by word, but I do remember him saying, "The Lord told me to tell you that you are a woman waving the banner of freedom." He said because I had been set free and delivered from much, I was now to take other women to the well of God's Word so they too could drink. All that I needed, God would provide. The power of God hit me as I stumbled over rows of chairs.

You are a woman waving the banner of freedom.

Shortly after the service, the prophet encouraged me to obey God because He sent him to deliver that word to me. Immediately, my husband, with whom I had been sharing my dreams and visions, looked at me and said, "Obey God! This man confirmed what God has been telling you, and we have never seen him in our lives." I went home and began to cry out to the Lord. I also asked for forgiveness because the Lord had been speaking to me about teaching women, but I was pushing it back!

God sent His prophet John Harke to openly deliver this word to me in a church full of witnesses. I was ready to surrender all. The Holy Spirit ministered to me that God had chosen me to help set hurting women free. I was an evangelist speaking all over the place at different churches. I really didn't want to stop to gather women, but I always had a heart and burden of compassion for them. Truth is I didn't want to deal with women. You really have to be anointed and called by God to deal with many women. However, the Lord had given me instructions, and I had to obey.

WWTBOF

The first thing the Holy Spirit told me was to get the cassette tape from the soundman of the church and go back over the prophetic message. I would find the instructions for the women's conference on it. I contacted the soundman at the church, and he had the prophetic word given to me on a cassette tape. I listened closely to the instructions and the name of the ministry. They were all there, "Women Waving the Banner of Freedom."

In 2003, the women's ministry was birthed with over five hundred women attending our WWTBOF conference in Long Beach at the Hilton Hotel. I didn't really know what I was doing. I was simply obeying the Lord step-by-step as hundreds of women came and left with life-changing testimonies of how God had delivered and set them free! It was amazing. Hundreds of women waved victory

Me and my spiritual daughter Evang. Sharrel, my first armorbearer for over 20 years – 1999

flags with tears streaming down their faces. All I could do was cry. I felt so inadequate that God could use such a nobody like me to help set hundreds of women free.

After a few conferences, I invited Prophet Harke to speak because he was the man God had entrusted to deliver the word to me that would change thousands of lives. I call him one of my fathers of the faith.

Me in a white robe ministering to hundreds of women in red – 2006

WWTBOF is now about to host its 17th annual conference. Who would have ever thought God would use this girl from the ghettos of Watts, raised in a dysfunctional home with childhood trauma, illiteracy, abandonment issues, drug addiction, prostitution, physical and mental abuse, and the death of her five-year-old daughter to ever impact so many lives for His glory? Today, I still see Prophet Harke as a true prophet of God. My husband and I are pastoring a wonderful congregation by the name of New Region For Christ. From time to time, we still call in Prophet Harke and his wife Meleana to speak.

We must all remember God takes the foolish things to confound the wise. Shortly after the first WWTBOF, the Lord spoke a word to me and said, "I have chosen you to be a mother in Zion. I want you to spiritually nurture broken women through the Word of God. I am sending you many spiritual daughters." Soon they came, one by one. The first ones were Sharrel, Theressa (Peaches), and Jamesha. These were the first ladies I mentored and trained in the things of God. Today they are powerful women preachers, teachers, and prayer warriors for the kingdom of God. Shortly after these ladies were birthed, others came from everywhere one by one as the Lord led them.

WWTBOF Ladies in red with gift baskets – 2009

WWTBOF Ladies in red receiving certificates of completion – 2009

WWTBOF Ladies in red with gift baskets – 2009

Today some are pastoring churches and evangelizing the world: for example, Prophetess Kelinda and her husband, Apostle Reginald D. Rice Sr., founder of Kingdom Faith Ministries Intl. Inc. There is also Prophetess/Pastor Aneesha M. Ross of Divine Favor International Ministries. Others are still standing strong for God right in the marketplace.

A valuable lesson I learned early on in ministry is you cannot have this level of anointing without the adversary being near. Spiritual warfare is a part of ministry as well. If you think the enemy is going to

TAKE THE WOMEN TO THE WELL

sit back and say, "Go on! Lead as many people as you like to the Lord," you are mistaken. He will not. He will fight relentlessly to stop you.

Mentor Me

The Lord instructed us to expand the ministry by teaching and training the women for ministry through our Mentor Me program. In this program, we build stronger women God's way. At our yearly conference, each lady receives a certificate and gift basket of completion. We teach women how to appropriately engage in ministry with love, passion, and integrity.

Mentor Me ladies in white T-shirts and blue jeans – 2009

Hundreds of women have traveled through the WWTBOF ministry and Mentor Me training programs. Today they are doing great exploits for the kingdom of God. I wish I could name them all, but they know who they are. Plus, I don't want to leave anyone out. More importantly, God knows your name and labor for the kingdom.

Looking back, I thank God for all of them. Many have sacrificed greatly to see other women delivered. Together we have ministered to women in homeless shelters and provided necessities for women in gift boxes. We have visited women's prisons weekly, going behind bars, ministering the good news, and praying for them. Several women gave their lives to the Lord.

A few WWTBOF Coordinators – ladies in white – 2015

The year 2020 will mark our 17th annual WWTBOF women's conference. Women come to WWTBOF to have an encounter with the Lord, be healed, restored, and taught the Word of God. They are educated on relevant topics. None of this has come easy. It came at a high price and great sacrifice. One may ask why do it then? I say, "If only one woman can experience the deliverance and freedom I have throughout my transformation, it's worth it all!" Never shy away from what the Lord has called you to do because of spiritual warfare. Real kingdom visionaries continue to build despite demonic warfare. The Lord takes no pleasure in those who draw back!

Nehemiah continued to build the walls of Jerusalem with one hand on the wall building and the other with a sword ready to fight. Many people often say, "Well, I don't have the education or the money to do ministry." However, I say, "Where there is vision, God will always give provision." I have come to learn in my twenty-five years of ministry that God is not looking for perfect people. Rather, He's looking for willing and obedient people who will say, "Yes, Lord."

Seventeen years ago, all I had was a "Yes, Lord." WWTBOF has helped many women to walk in liberty and freedom from the chains that once held them in captivity. God took a flawed vessel and broke it beyond recognition for a greater purpose than I could have ever imagined. Was I exempt from being hit by the enemy now that I was walking in destiny? No!

White Spot

Immediately after I said, "Yes, Lord," I woke up one morning with a white spot on my hand the size of a dime. Curious about what it was, I set a doctor's appointment and was diagnosed with vitiligo, a skin disorder. I was broken and crying hysterically. "You mean to tell me I'm losing my skin pigment?"

"Yes," the doctor said. He asked me if anyone else in my family had been diagnosed with vitiligo. The answer was yes. My maternal grandfather had it and my mother had a very small spot. Now me! I was not ready for this one, so I stood on my faith. I prayed. I cried. I prayed and I cried asking God why me. I told Him I had four other siblings with not a spot on them. Why me, Lord? As the spots continued to grow larger, the Lord sent me to read,

> *But he said to me, "My grace is sufficient for you, for my power is made perfect in weakness." Therefore I will boast all the more gladly about my weaknesses, so that Christ's power may rest on me. That is why, for Christ's sake, I delight in weaknesses, in insults, in hardships, in persecutions, in difficulties. For when I am weak, then I am strong. (2 Corinthians 12:9-10, NIV)*

Be encouraged; God doesn't make mistakes.

Many years had passed, and I realized God was not going to supernaturally remove the vitiligo. It was a thorn in my flesh I would have to learn to live with until He healed me. To my surprise, the vitiligo opened me up to an inner beauty I didn't know I had. I disconnected from the outer beauty that was superficial and temporal and began to operate from my inner beauty, which was genuine.

I did my research and found out you can live as long and healthy as anyone else with your vitiligo. Vitiligo is a skin disorder in which white patches develop on the skin. Any location on the body can be affected. Most people with vitiligo have white patches on many areas. The skin doesn't have its characteristic color because it has lost its melanin. For some reason, the pigment cells known as melanocytes have been destroyed. No one knows exactly why this happens as vitiligo affects all races equally; it's just more noticeable in people of color.

WWTBOF Coordinators – ladies in white – 2016

So I have learned to embrace my vitiligo and allow God to use it for His glory as well. I could help someone struggling in that area. While vitiligo is not contagious, many people are misinformed and ignorant about it. If you or someone you know has vitiligo, you are uniquely beautiful as God created you to be. You can live a long, healthy life as well.

When I look at my hands, I realize how uniquely different I am in a good way! Lots of people with this skin disorder deal with shame and embarrassment. Many hibernate from society because of the way people look at them. But you must heal from those emotions quickly; otherwise, the enemy will use it as a weapon against you.

I recall a prayer meeting we had at our church. Usually, I wear makeup on my hands to cover the vitiligo spots so that it's not a distraction when I'm ministering. However, this particular night I didn't wear it, which was unusual. As the service progressed, the Spirit of the Lord instructed me to testify about my deliverance from vitiligo shame. As I spoke, a young lady came forth crying about having vitiligo and the shame she experienced. I prayed with her; she was healed from the shame she was struggling with. Be encouraged; God doesn't make mistakes. What the enemy meant for evil, He is going to use for your good whatever your situation is.

Beauty Is Only Skin Deep

Without a doubt, I'm a humbler, more loving, kind, and compassionate person now than I ever was before. My skin was flawless all the way until my thirties, but I was so full of pride. Some of the most beautiful people outside can be the ugliest people inside. There's an old song that says, "Beauty is only skin deep!" And I must add, "It's fading away every day." Whatever challenges you may be facing, surround yourself with people who genuinely love you. My biggest supporters are my husband, family, and a few genuine friends. For years they were very mindful of my vitiligo and would make sure I was covered until I was ready to expose it. Their love for me is unconditional.

I've had vitiligo for over twenty years, and it still amazes me when people say, "You are beautiful." I have come to terms with this condition. I now realize that one day this physical house (body) in which I live will return to the dirt. My focus is now on the inner beauty, which I display and allow the light to shine bright!

Yes, I have suffered many things in my life. Still, I say "Yes, Lord," so I may see others healed and set free in every area of their lives.

WWTBOF was never a good idea.
It has always been a God idea.

CHAPTER 13

BROKEN BEYOND RECOGNITION

I have learned that God takes the foolish things to confound the wise. I am the foolish thing! He used all my hurts, pains, bad choices, and issues to help break me. I could see clearly that what the enemy meant for evil against me, God was using for my good. The day I realized I had been broken beyond recognition was when an old friend of mine was getting married and invited me to her bridal shower. I thought about not attending as it had been some years since I had seen many of my associates from back in the day. But I decided to go.

Many of them kept asking me one by one in surprise, "Kathy, is that you?"

"Yes, it is," I said. I found myself saying that over and over throughout the evening to each one who remembered me from back in the day.

They kept saying, "You look like you, but you don't sound or act like you. Something is different about you!" I still remember their faces as they looked at me in astonishment.

They couldn't put it into words, so I helped them to understand that I was a Christian now. Having heard that declaration, they looked at me with even more amazement in their eyes. Then I realized I had been gracefully broken beyond recognition and didn't fit in anymore. I had been broken by God, so He could take me to a new level in Him. I left the bridal shower. As I got into my car tears flowed down my face representing the inner work of the Holy Spirit that had begun in me. Then the Spirit of God began to minister to me on my way home.

He said, "It wasn't that they didn't physically recognize you, daughter. Rather, they didn't recognize your spirit." Wow! Before my spiritual makeover, I was a mess. I wore a cute mask on the outside, but inside I was loud, prideful, angry, bitter, hateful, and arrogant. I would handle every issue with anger and violence. Now the fruit of the Spirit takes priority in my life: love, joy, peace, patience, kindness, goodness, faithfulness, gentleness, and self-control. This is the beauty of brokenness, to walk in the fruit of the Spirit that brings joy to the lives of others.

When we become new creatures in Christ Jesus, the Bible says old things are passed away and behold all things become new. I was now walking in the newness of Jesus Christ, and many couldn't recognize me.

The Cost of Shame
Sometimes the enemy fights against us by bringing up our history and bombarding us with thoughts of unworthiness and shame. One of the unfortunate things about shame is it puts you in a place of isolation from people who really care about you. Sometimes, God will send people to help pull you out of a situation that is way beyond your control. But if you allow shame and pride to hinder you, then you will never know what could have become of it.

I remember finally speaking with Dee-Dee, my best friend from high school friend. I was now walking with the Lord Jesus Christ and having Bible Studies in my home helping people come into the knowledge of this Savior Who had set me free. One day in 1998 as I was preparing for bible study my phone ringed. It was a mutual friend of Dee-Dee and mines. She said, "Hello, I have Dee-Dee on the phone. I immediately began to scream for joy that my friend was on the phone wanting to talk to me. It had been some 20 years since I had talked to her and now here we were so happy to be reconnecting. We were setting up some plans to see one another and catch up on old times. But sometime in September, I received a call that Dee-Dee had passed away. We never did get a chance to see each other again. Hurt and devastated, I cried and prayed for her family and friends as we all had lost a precious jewel. Rest well Dee-Dee.

Sweeping Up the Pieces
God is constantly working to bring us all to the place of brokenness in a good way. It is not to hurt us but to help us! God will never give up on us until we are broken. He consistently works with us using all kinds of methods. Sometimes there is a sudden breaking. Other times it can be daily trials, hard circumstances, physical problems, and all sorts of things to bring us to a place of brokenness. But be sure, He's not only in the business of lovingly breaking us but also

sweeping up all the broken pieces and molding them back together for His greater purpose.

The Lord is close to the brokenhearted and saves those who are crushed in spirit. (Psalm 34:18)

My sacrifice, O God, is a broken spirit; a broken and contrite heart, you God will not despise. (Psalm 51:17)

God will never despise or walk away from people who live with broken spirits and contrite hearts. I tell people all the time, I was filled with pride. If you are filled with pride, get rid of it before it gets rid of you. Pride is believing the problem is always someone else's. Pride is a prison that demonstrates anger, hurt, and foolishness, while keeping away the effects of conviction, humility, forgiveness, and reconciliation.

Pride goes before destruction, and a haughty spirit before a fall. (Proverbs 16:18)

Pride is disobedience to God's command to love Him above all else and love our neighbors as ourselves. If you are dealing with pride, pray and ask God to reveal it to you and remove it from your heart and mind, so you can live a Christlike life.

You may feel as though your life is full of flaws and failures, and God would never use you. However, as I said earlier, God takes the *foolish things* of the world to confound the wise. It's not too late for you!

BROKEN BEYOND RECOGNITION 139

Imperfect People

God has always chosen imperfect people who don't have picture-perfect pasts. Let me give you a few examples:

- God chose Rahab for a major role in the Bible; she was a prostitute
- God chose Ruth to be one of Jesus' ancestors, even though Ruth was childless, a widow, and a foreigner
- God chose Moses to represent Him as His spokesperson. Moses had a serious stuttering problem, not to mention, he murdered a man
- God chose Abraham to be the father of faith, even though Abraham had a serious problem with lying
- God chose Noah, who many thought was perfect. However, after the flood, Noah got so drunk he passed out completely naked
- Joseph came from a family so dysfunctional his own brothers sold him into slavery. Yet God chose Joseph to save His people from famine
- God chose David, who was an adulterer, to be a leader over His people

The bottom line is God has a history of choosing imperfect people with problems. So if you have flaws, failures, and weaknesses, guess what? They don't disqualify you.

God's strength is your power over any of your weaknesses. Remain humble, and He will use you to minister to others. Perhaps you've struggled with something. God is

I actually like who I am today!

going to lead you to recovery so you can encourage people in bondage as an example of how He can bring supernatural healing to their lives as well. Trust the process! God will use it all. By the way, I actually like who I am today! But it was a process, and God is still working on me. God has used many of my circumstances to break me.

Benz to Bikes

I recall one particular incident God used to break my pride—and there were many. But this one hit hard as my husband and I had lost our only car to repossession because we couldn't keep up the payments. Have you ever been there? We were new Christians, and it seemed as if we were having trial after trial. After the car was repossessed, we still had to be at church and my husband still had to be at work, so a couple of times friends would give us a ride.

One Saturday we were low on food and needed to get to the market, but no one was available to give us a ride. My husband looked at me and said, "We have two bikes in the garage; we are going to ride them to the market to get food for our kids."

Immediately, I said, "No, I am not riding no bike to the market and have to ride back with a bunch of bags! What will people think of me? I'm used to driving Mercedes-Benz and Jaguars. What will I look like shopping on a bike?"

My husband said, "I don't care what you are used to or what you will look like. Right now, we are going to the market to get our children some food. Let's go!"

He pulled the bikes out of the garage and told me to get on one of them. I pouted all the way to the market. We left the bikes outside and began to shop. My husband was shopping as if we had a car outside to put all the food in. There were so many bags. I asked him where we were going to put them. Gently, he said, "Watch me." He tied them to the handlebars of my bike and his.

"Oh, no!" I said. "All these bags… we look a hot mess."

He said, "Let's go!"

I began to cry and tried to hide from people on my way back home. Suddenly a car drove by blowing its horn. And, yes, it was someone I knew from back in the day. The person asked if I was OK or needed help. I said I was OK as she drove off. Another one said, "Hey, Kathy, is that you, girl? Do you need help? Where is your car? What are you doing with all those bags?"

"No, I don't need help!"

I was embarrassed, crying, and pumping hard to catch up with my husband. I got home, went into my bedroom, and began crying out to God. He revealed to me that I was full of pride, and He was going to destroy it. He made sure everyone I didn't want to see, saw me!

After a few weeks, Elder Candler asked my husband if he wanted to use his van. It wasn't new, but it ran very well, and we could use it until we got a car. My husband was very grateful, but all I could think about was whether it was new. Sundays, we would gather the kids and head off to church. As soon as I thought someone recognized me, I would duck my head in the van. And the Lord said to me, "You are still prideful."

Suddenly, the van broke down by the side of the road. Now we were walking. My husband called Elder Cardell, who said the van was running perfectly fine when he let us use it. But the Lord was after me and that pride. No one could help us, and we didn't have the money to buy a car. For six months, we walked everywhere. I cried out to the Lord and repented for being so ungrateful and prideful.

A Lesson in Humility

About a week later, my cousin Loretta called me and said, "Hey, cousin, I heard you need a car. Well, I have an old Toyota hatchback. It's nothing fancy like you are used to driving, but it runs well, and you can have it. You don't have to give me anything." Before she could finish the sentence, I said, "Yes, cousin! Yes!" I was crying and thanking God that He had broken me down to a place of humility and gratefulness.

We were just as happy as if we were driving something new.

When she brought the car over to our house, it was old and needed a paint job. It was nothing fancy at all, but I didn't care! I was grateful just to have anything to get us around. My husband washed it and put some Armor All on the tires. We were just as happy as if we were driving something new.

God is amazing! He knows just what it took to break me. About a year later, God blessed me and my husband with good jobs, and we were able to buy a new car. We gave the Toyota hatchback to someone else who needed a car. After two years, they gave it to someone else as a blessing. I really learned some valuable lessons in that whole situation. One of them is to never think of yourself more highly than you ought to. Here are some key verses:

- *God humbles those who exalt themselves (Isaiah 10:12; Daniel 4:20)*
- *God hates haughty eyes (Proverbs 6:16)*
- *God hates a proud look (Proverbs 6:16-17)*
- *God hates the proud in heart (Proverbs 16:5; 8:13)*
- *Pride is practical atheism (Psalm 10:4)*
- *Jesus Christ models humility (Philippians 2:6-11)*
- *God exalts the humble (James 4:10)*

Jesus Christ humbled Himself so He could rightly be exalted.

Therefore God has highly exalted him and bestowed on him the name that is above every name, so that at the name of Jesus every knee should bow, in heaven and on earth and under the earth, and every tongue confess that Jesus Christ is Lord, to the glory of God the Father.
(Philippians 2:9-11, ESV)

Look at Jesus. He humbled Himself, so who are we to think we don't have to be humble. I often tell people, "I don't care how much wealth and material possessions you have or the titles you hold. Remain humble because those things can be here today and gone tomorrow. After all, we came into this world with nothing, and we will leave with nothing. It's better to humble yourself than for God to humble you.

> *Humble yourselves, therefore, under God's mighty hand, that he may lift you up in due time. (1 Peter 5:6, NIV)*
>
> *And he said, "Naked I came from my mother's womb, and naked shall I return. The Lord gave, and the Lord has taken away; blessed be the name of the Lord."*
> *(Job 1:21, ESV)*

Once I began walking in real humility, doors of opportunity opened for me. Humility is an attractive virtue. It's the complete emptying of oneself before God and others.

CHAPTER 14

HE GAVE ME BEAUTY. I GAVE HIM ASHES

Beauty effects are in every mark of the ashes. The ashes will fall away; they don't stay forever. God's greatness and glory will shine through all the brokenness and flaws that we've struggled through. I'm so much better today because the light of Christ shines in my heart. I have given Him all the ashes that used to hold me in captivity.

Sometimes our hopes and dreams can turn into ashes of disappointment, but God loves us and wants us to live the life He designed for us. He made us in our mothers' wombs and fashioned us with purpose. No matter how much we despise the person we see in the mirror, God loves that person. He loved us so much that while we were unrighteous, unholy, and sinners unworthy of His goodness, He sent His one and only begotten Son. He did so to trade our sins for His forgiveness, our unrighteousness for His righteousness, our scarred and dirty past for a new life in Him, and our old identity as slaves of sin to children of God called to live in His kingdom (Romans 5:8; John 3:16; 1 John 4:10; 2 Corinthians 5:21; Colossians 1:13). He made the trade on the cross of Calvary. Yes, He loves you! (Psalm 139:13-17)

To appoint unto them that mourn in Zion, to give unto them beauty for ashes, the oil of joy for mourning, the garment of praise for the spirit of heaviness; that they might be called trees of righteousness, the planting of the LORD, that he might be glorified. (Isaiah 61:3)

Ministering to hundreds of women at my cousin Bishop John M. Richardson's church New Journey – 2006

In the Bible, it was customary for people to sit in ashes or cover themselves with ashes to express their pain and grief (2 Samuel 13:19). It showed sorrow for a public disaster (Esther 4:1) or heartache connected to repentance from sin (Jonah 3:5-7). Ashes were linked to pain, loss, sorrow, and suffering from the struggles of the flesh.

If He did it for me, He can do it for you.

Today we can find hope and encouragement in Isaiah 61:3. God is still just and merciful. He forgives, heals, and restores. Beauty for ashes is God's promise that He delivered us from our troubles through Jesus Christ so we can break free from our fears, sorrows, worries, and false conclusions about ourselves and others. You can overcome your struggles! If He did it for me, He can do it for you as well.

> *What an amazing exchange! God takes the ashes of our sorrows, pain, despair, hurt, and tears then gives us the beauty of joy, healing, peace of mind, prosperity, and blessings. You too can trust the Lord and watch beauty come from ashes. To grant to those who mourn in Zion— to give them a beautiful headdress instead of ashes, the oil of gladness instead of mourning, the garment of praise instead of a faint spirit; that they may be called oaks of righteousness, the planting of the Lord, that he may be glorified. (Isaiah 61:3, ESV)*

You have loved righteousness and hated wickedness; therefore God, your God, has anointed you with the oil of gladness beyond your companions. (Hebrews 1:9, ESV)

The Spirit of the Lord God is upon me, because the Lord has anointed me to bring good news to the poor; he has sent me to bind up the brokenhearted, to proclaim liberty to the captives, and the opening of the prison to those who are bound. (Isaiah 61:1, ESV)

And this is the key to the ashes that cover our days in this life. The deep truth that shines through every bit of our grief, pain, and sin is this: Jesus Christ came to bring hope. Christ came to bring forth beauty from ashes!

CHAPTER 15

YOU CAN MAKE IT! I DID

Life is full of challenges, and although I have come a mighty long way, God is still working on me. My advice to you is to stay close to Him. Be determined and remember you have as much right to be here as anyone else! You may not add up to what success is in the eyes of others, but it doesn't mean you're not successful in the eyes of God. Let go and let God!

He knows everything about us because He created us. Nothing is hidden from the Lord. The Bible says, "Weeping may endure for a night, but joy cometh in the morning" (Psalm 30:5). All our pain, sorrow, and suffering are transparent before God. He takes our shattered, broken pieces, sets them back up on the Potter's wheel, and molds us again. The Potter wants to put you back together again. You can make it!

Sometimes we feel discouraged and defeated. Things happen that cause us to tremble within the deepest parts of our souls, places where only God can give us comfort. God has promised to be with us at all times because we are His children. Don't be so hard on yourself. God is in full control.

We Are Forgiven

For He has rescued us from the dominion of darkness and brought us into the kingdom of the Son he loves, in whom we have redemption, the forgiveness of sins.
(Colossians 1:13-14)

It might seem like the world has turned against you and all you can see at times are lots of problems, bad circumstances, and challenges before you. But, believe me, it's just a trial period. You must never faint, lose hope in yourself, or give in to the temptation to quit.

There hath no temptation taken you but such as is common to man: but God is faithful, who will not suffer you to be tempted above that ye are able; but will with the temptation also make a way to escape, that ye may be able to bear it. (1 Corinthians 10:1)

The Lord is my shepherd; I shall not want. He maketh me to lie down in green pastures: he leadeth me beside the still waters. He restoreth my soul: he leadeth me in the paths of righteousness for his name's sake. Yea, though I walk through the valley of the shadow of death, I will fear no evil: for thou art with me; thy rod and staff they comfort me. Thou prepare a table before me in the presence of mine enemies; thou anointest my head with oil; my cup runneth over. Surely goodness and mercy shall follow me all the days of my life: and I will dwell in the house of the Lord for ever. (Psalm 23:1-6)

I will not be afraid, for You are close beside me. Every Christian learns that life's journey is not always easy, smooth, or perfect. We will all have our valley experiences. However, you are not a permanent resident in your valley experience; God is always at work to bring you through.

Therefore, you can completely trust Him whenever you're at the crossroads where you are forced to face life's trials, and you are at the point of not knowing what to do. Fall on your knees and call upon the name of the Lord. He will show up!

Come As You Are

Today I tell those considering coming to the Lord to come just as you are. Don't get caught up with religious people and all their rules. Come to Jesus just as you are. He loves you and desires to have a relationship with you. I'm cut from a different cloth, and religious people have a problem with me because I didn't come into Christianity with a perfect "done no wrong" testimony but with a broken and contrite heart. I have learned that Jesus is not concerned with how perfect you are but how hungry you are for Him.

Thank you for reading my book! I hope you found something helpful and useful in it. I also hope you enjoyed reading my stories. I would really appreciate if you could leave a review wherever you bought the book. Thank you in advance.

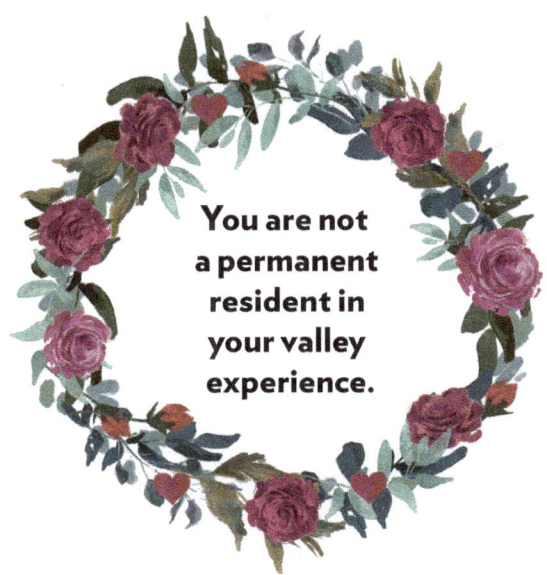

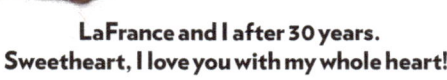

LaFrance and I after 30 years.
Sweetheart, I love you with my whole heart!

SPECIAL ACKNOWLEDGMENTS

*To
my wonderful God-sent
husband, the fudge on my sundae,
the king of our castle, my ride-or-die,
LaFrance A. Simpson. You have gently and
patiently healed my broken heart by loving me
past my pain. Boo, you have outdone them all!
I am so honored to be your wife. We have traveled
through some rough times, but we fought it out
ten toes down and back to back! It has been a
wonderful journey loving you. I never knew
a love like this before. Thank you for
restoring a wounded woman.
Your "good thing,"
Kat.*

To my amazing and wonderful children who have forever changed my life for the better: Kuleshia (rest well, beautiful), Anthony, Kierra, Kamerra, Joshua, and LaFrance Jr. You have all given me a reason to fight and live! Your unconditional love has kept me from giving up.

You guys have given me the strength I didn't know I had. Each one of you is uniquely different and special to me in your own way. Never depart from your faith in Jesus Christ. He has traveled a long way with our family, and He will see us through. Live your best life because the fruit of my womb is blessed! I love you all dearly, Momma.

To my siblings who came through the childhood struggle with me: Ronald, Antoinette, Cynthia, and Louis (Papa), we have always had each other's back no matter what. And we made it. When the odds of life were against us trying to destroy our lives, we held tight to one another for strength and comfort. My love for the four of you is immeasurable; only God knows our unbreakable bond. I wish you all the very best in your life journey. Always remember we are a strong, loving, compassionate, forgiving, and God-fearing people who give and demand respect. God's hand has been with the five of us since day one, so always give Him all the glory for your accomplishments. May your latter be greater than your former. We are and will always be "The Five Who Survived." Endless love from big Sis.

Christian Living Book Publishing, you are amazing! As a first-time author, I was skeptical. My nerves oftentimes wanted me to turn around and rethink publishing this book. But after meeting Kimberly Stewart, I was hopeful and full of excitement throughout the process. Kimberly motivated and inspired me by pulling out the best in me. Her creativity is an anointing given only by God. Christian Living Books is very professional and patient. I highly recommend them for anyone looking for a great publishing company. Thank you CLB. I am so appreciative.

To Lady Vicki L. Kemp, I'm still in awe of our divine relationship. It is an honor to know such an amazing person. From day one, you gave me your very candid and honest advice. You shared truths and gave me a fresh reason to push when I felt like letting go.

Your inspiring words kept me holding on. Thank you, my sister, for lifting a sister up. You are a real one.

To my "Glam Team," you guys are amazing! Thanks for your expertise and creativity. I'm so appreciative of you all. Much love.

*Pic: @wanthy_d
*MUA: @jolisarena
*Hair: @hairbykitkat
*Fashion Stylist: @facesofkamerra

ACKNOWLEDGMENTS

To the people who helped me along the way and taught me some valuable lessons:

To my parents, Louis F. Elam III and Gwendolyn Elam (RIP). I truly believe that in the depths of your hearts your intentions were to do the right thing. However, somewhere along the way you lost your focus and opened the door to substance abuse, which played a major part in your poor decision making. But today I have no regrets or unforgiveness in my heart toward you. All the pain you caused your children made the five of us some of the most amazing people to ever walk this earth. I love you. You are forgiven.

To my grandparents, Louis F. Elam Jr. and Dorothy L. Elam (RIP), for loving and nurturing five broken children. What you did in taking on the responsibility of five grandchildren after raising your own is incredible. Only God could have given you both the strength. Big Momma and Big Daddy, your love stopped the hemorrhaging in our hearts and gave us a chance to live. You will never be forgotten. Endless love.

To my auntie and uncle, Elder George and Eloise Richardson Sr. (RIP) of Bethel Church of God in Christ, you laid the spiritual foundation and planted the seed that would one day bring me full circle. I'm the woman of God I am today because of your love and God-like spirit of compassion for the underprivileged. You fulfilled James 1:27 in every way. Eternally grateful with love.

To Pastor Edward T. Robinson Sr. (RIP) and First Lady Ruby Robinson, my spiritual parents, thank you for your support and imparting the Word of God into my husband and me. Thank you for not only preaching and teaching it but living it before us. You both have been the example of what real Christians should look like. Your integrity spoke volumes to us. We love you forever.

To Evangelist Faylean Hillard, thank you, mother, for your support in teaching me how to walk in true holiness. Thanks for all the wisdom you have imparted over the years. I love you dearly.

To Elder Cardell and Cherie Candler, our spiritual mentors, wow! LaFrance and I love you both. Your light has always shone so brightly! Thank you for your patience and taking the time out with my husband and me. We are certain that we would not be who we are today without both of you. You guys taught us the Word of God in great depth. When we were just babies in Christ, you spoon-fed us. Today you oversee us as we shepherd a beautiful God-loving people at NRFC. We're so honored to have sat under your tutelage. We'll forever be grateful to you both for the spiritual guidance you have given to us for over twenty-five years and counting. Thank you. We love you both dearly.

To Dr. Vickie Lee (rest in the Lord) of S.O.V. Training Center, my mentor, I'm honored to have sat under your ministry, a ministry that taught me many spiritual truths. Your discernment to recognize the gift in me and to call it out was incredible. You trained and ordained me as an evangelist and said, "Always let the Holy Ghost lead you." I love and miss you.

To all my spiritual daughters and the many women I have mentored from WWTBOF, Mentor Me, True Love Waits, and NRFC. You ladies are amazing! You have co-labored with me, and now you are running the race that is set before you. Never give up on the prize! You will win if you continue to keep your eyes upon Jesus Christ, who is the Author and Finisher of our faith. We have done some great work together for the kingdom of God, and the work continues. Never walk away from the faith and sound doctrine of the biblical truths you have learned. Hold them dear and close to your heart. I love you ladies dearly.

THE FIVE WHO SURVIVED

Congratulations, Sis, on such a well-written book. The struggles we went through as children were very difficult and disturbing. However, your inspirational story will benefit others who may have faced those same or similar challenges. You are truly an inspiration to us all. I love you, Sis!

YOUR BROTHER, RONALD F. ELAM SR.

Congratulations, Sis! I am so proud of you and all you have accomplished. Our childhood struggles were real, but we made it! I know your book will be a blessing to many. It's time for your story to be heard. I love you dearly.

YOUR SISTER, ANTOINETTE ELAM MIMS

Congratulations, Sis, on the release of such an inspiring must-read book. You were chosen and God instructed you to share your life story. This book will give hope to inspire others who may have experienced similar struggles, so they may see how God changed you from your hurting childhood to the woman of God you are today. I'm trusting that if God can change Kathy, He can change me too. To God be the glory!

YOUR SISTER, CYNTHIA

I am pleased to endorse this "tell all" book in support of my oldest sister. She has personally supported me in all my endeavors in life. Although Kathy has been through many trials and tribulations, she has never wavered. Her faith has given her the strength to overcome obstacles. Through her perseverance that I've personally witnessed, I can sincerely say she has been through many hardships but has not let them destroy her. She is the true meaning of resilient.

YOUR BROTHER, LOUIS W. ELAM IV

ABOUT THE AUTHOR

Evangelist Katherine Elam Simpson was born and raised in the inner city of Watts, Los Angeles. Her childhood was filled with difficult times. It was the love she shared with her siblings that enabled her to cope with alcoholic and drug-addicted parents. Little did Katherine know that the Lord had a plan for her life. She credits her zeal for life to her grandparents, the late Louis F. Elam Jr. and Dorothy L. Elam. Their unconditional love snatched her from the gates of hell. Katherine credits her spiritual walk to her uncle and aunt, the late Elder George and Elouise Richardson (Bethel Church of God in Christ) for the seed they planted in 1973.

Still wounded and hurting from her childhood trauma, Katherine became involved in a lifestyle that nearly killed her. In 1986, she experienced the unexpected death of her five-year-old daughter, Kuleshia. The Lord began the process of turning her life around.

Years later Katherine rededicated her life to the Lord at Trinity Chapel of Compton, California, under the direction of Pastor Edward T. Robinson Sr.

Katherine answered the call from the Lord by enrolling in the Saints of Value World Ministries Training Center, where she graduated as an ordained minister. Continuing her education at Esther Mallett International Bible University in 2002, Katherine graduated with a Bachelor of Arts degree in biblical theology.

Katherine is a vibrant and charismatic minister. She is noted for her soul-stirring messages and practical application of Christian principles. Through her evangelistic messages at church events, revivals, women's conferences, and Sunday morning worship services as the co-pastor of New Region For Christ, the Lord uses her to preach the gospel to hurting, neglected, and spiritually dying people. She brings a message of hope that "you can make it." Katherine has been endorsed by many great and influential leaders including her spiritual father and mentor, the late Edward T. Robinson Sr. and Elder Cardell Candler, respectively.

Aside from her ministerial duties, Katherine is the proud wife of Pastor LaFrance Simpson. Together they are the parents of five wonderful children. She is also the founder of Women Waving the Banner of Freedom (WWTBOF). This ministry conducts annual conferences and has a thriving mentorship program that "Builds stronger women God's way." Katherine says, "Where He sends me, I'll go!" A woman on a mission, she is uniquely articulate and highly respected. Her ministry is setting a precedence of excellence, power, and grace.

Connect with Katherine
Email: Kgirls4@icloud.com
Instagram: firstladyksimpson
Facebook: Katherine Elam Simpson

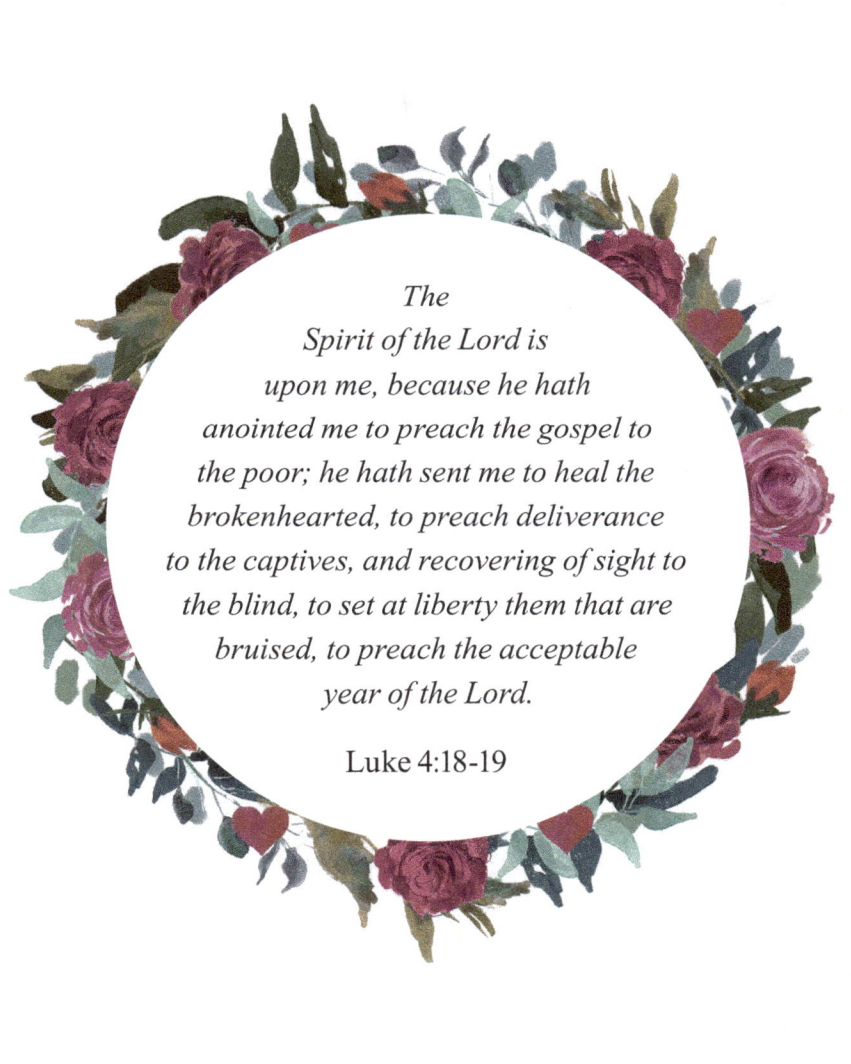

The Spirit of the Lord is upon me, because he hath anointed me to preach the gospel to the poor; he hath sent me to heal the brokenhearted, to preach deliverance to the captives, and recovering of sight to the blind, to set at liberty them that are bruised, to preach the acceptable year of the Lord.

Luke 4:18-19

www.ingramcontent.com/pod-product-compliance
Lightning Source LLC
Chambersburg PA
CBHW040303170426
43194CB00021B/2883